MW01530392

A Modern Guide to Astrology
The Only Astrology Book You Will Ever Need

Table of Contents

© Copyright 2019 - All rights reserved.

The contents of this book may not be reproduced, duplicated or transmitted without direct written permission from the author.

Under no circumstances will any legal responsibility or blame be held against the publisher for any reparation, damages, or monetary loss due to the information herein, either directly or indirectly.

<u>Legal Notice:</u>

You cannot amend, distribute, sell, use, quote or paraphrase any part or the content within this book without the consent of the author.

<u>Disclaimer Notice:</u>

Please note the information contained within this document is for educational and entertainment purposes only. No warranties of any kind are expressed or implied. Readers acknowledge that the author is not engaging in the rendering of legal, financial, medical or professional advice. Please consult a licensed professional before attempting any techniques outlined in this book.

By reading this document, the reader agrees that under no circumstances are is the author responsible for any losses, direct or indirect, which are incurred as a result of the use of information contained within

this document, including, but not limited to, —
errors, omissions, or inaccuracies.

Introduction

Thank you for buying this book, and I hope you will find it informative and useful.

Astrology is one of the most complex and exciting things in the world. After all, who does not want to know what their future holds for them? If you are interested in astrology, this book is sure to help you understand it and use it in your day-to-day life.

Astrology can be defined as the study of the influence of heavenly objects on our lives. These celestial objects include the stars, planets, asteroids, satellites, etc. The positions of these elements at the time of an individual's birth (and not their conception) determines a lot of things about them and their lives. For instance, astrology can be used to understand a person's personality, his or her attitude and aptitude, their feelings, and their emotions as well. It can also show their romantic relationships and can predict certain things, including financial and professional life.

Many people know of astrology thanks to the 'horoscope', which has become a fixture in many magazines and dailies. They also know their zodiac signs and the traits associated with them. This is sun sign astrology on which most of these newspaper horoscopes are based. It is the most straightforward and easy to understand any form of astrology, but it is also the most limited form. The results and predictions of this form of astrology are often confusing and may prove to be wrong, as well. Its simplistic nature has made popular, but due to its problems, many people now believe that astrology is fake.

It is possible to get accurate readings from astrology, but you need to have a lot more information than just your sun sign. A trained astrologer will check many different aspects, including the placement and positions of planets in your birth-chart. Planets, signs, and their positions can be used to create a far better and more accurate reading. Along with these elements, an astrologer studies the angles, houses, and the complexities formed due to them to understand the personality, the past, the present, and the future of an individual.

There are many different schools of astrology. Almost all ancient cultures practiced some form of divination and astrology. Most of these practices have been combined to form modern western astrology. Other forms of astrology that are still being practiced include Chinese, Vedic, and Tibetan astrology.

This book will only focus on Western astrology, as it is the most widely practiced type. This book will try to answer all your queries regarding this subject. Now let us enter the world of astrology and zodiac!

Chapter One: Basics of Astrology

Before moving on to the complex parts of astrology, it is necessary to understand its basics. This chapter will try to address all the basics of astrology and zodiac.

As said earlier, there are many different schools of astrology that are being practiced even now. Western astrology is one of the most popular schools of astrology. But even western astrology can be divided into many subsections on the basis of practices, methods, and results. Some astrologers divide astrology on the basis of results as follows:

Mundane Astrology – This section is used to understand world events. It can also be used to predict national and international affairs, including financial upheavals and wars.

Interrogatory Astrology- This branch has many subsections, but it generally deals with specific predictions and things related to particular objects in the concerned person's life.

Natal Astrology – Natal astrology is the most common form of astrology. Natal astrology uses the birthplace, date, and time of a person's birth to understand their personality and make predictions about their present and future. It believes that the stars above reflect the life below. This book will focus on natal astrology and how you can use it in your day-to-day life.

Astrologers and Data

The most commonly known sign is the sun sign. This sign is determined by the position of the Sun at the time of the birth of the individual. This concept may seem a bit odd because the Sun does not move, and it does not 'enter' anything per se. For this purpose, astrologers use the 'celestial sphere.' A celestial sphere is a giant sphere in which all the things in space exist. It is used to make measurements and calculate things. Astrologers and astronomers both use it.

As the Earth moves around completing its orbit, the Sun seems to move across the Celestial Sphere. This path of the Sun is known as the ecliptic. According to calculations, the Sun moves around 1 degree on the ecliptic every day. This ecliptic is offset from Earth's axis of rotation by approximately 23.5 degrees. This degree is essential as it is the reason behind seasons and the varying amount of sunlight that we receive.

The position of the Sun is determined using three things: the time of your birth, the place of your birth, and the astrological system that you use. Ancient astrologers were the first to figure this out. They did this by observing the rising and setting of the Sun. Thus, if a person says that he or she is a 'Cancer,' then that means that the Sun was in the Cancer constellation when they were born.

Generally, astrologers divide the ecliptic into 12 zones. Each of these zones has a distinct name, but they often do not line up the constellations. This practice is known as the sidereal zodiac. It was first discovered and developed around 400 BCE. Some astrologers also use the method of the tropical zodiac. In this method, the position of the signs is connected with the seasons. Both these methods used to produce identical results around 2000 years ago, but now the constellations have shifted in the sky, and the results too have changed significantly. This change happened due to precession.

Astrology and Signs

An astrologer starts the reading of any subject by first analyzing their date of birth. Along with the date of birth, the astrologer may often need the time of birth and the place of birth, as well.

Once this data is collected, the next step is to figure out the positions of various planets.

Astrological planets are different from normal planets. You will find more about planets and other celestial bodies in astrology in the next chapter. The position of the planets can be calculated accurately using scientific knowledge regarding the movements of planets and mathematical models. It is easy to calculate these positions to a certain extent, after which it becomes more and more difficult.

Like signs, each planet has its own influences, characteristics, and other varied aspects. How this influence is seen on the subject depends on the planet, its position, the sign, and the position of other planets as well. The combinations and permutations of these varied factors are almost infinite, and thus, a different astrologer can come up with different results and predictions even if they use the same system.

What Can Astrology Do?

Astrology is not magic; it is a kind of science that can be used to see things and understand them. Astrology can tell you a lot about yourself. Horoscopes often proclaim that they can predict the personality, future events, and the present of people. Along with this, astrology can also help you with your relationships and can help you make important decisions as well. While some astrologers do indulge in 'soothsaying' and 'divination,' many modern astrologers avoid doing so and stick to the 'personal advice' section instead.

A total personal reading is often extremely detailed and contains a lot of information regarding various celestial bodies, astrological phenomenon, their relationships, and how they can affect the individual. These readings are, in a way, a full psychological profile that helps you to make proper decisions. It includes things such as your love life, how you interact with people in your personal, professional, and social life, etc. It also contains information about your work, your behavior, and your overall attitude about life and other things. A good astrological reading can bring all the elements of your personality together and shed light on them. You can then use this reading to understand more about yourself. The more you understand yourself, the better you will become.

History of Astrology

Most of the early astrological systems were associated with seasons, weather patterns, rains, and crops. This was due to the fact that early human beings did not understand celestial phenomena such as eclipses, movements of planets, etc. Instead, they came up with stories that they believed explained these phenomena. These stories were passed from generation to generation for thousands of years. Stars and other celestial bodies became gods. Their apparent shapes became religious symbols. Looking at the ancient cultures, it can be surely said that almost all of them had some sort of scientific system that was used to study the patterns and movements of stars. Back in the day, astronomy and astrology were both the same. Astronomers worked as astrologers and vice versa. They used to observe and study the celestial bodies, and then they used these studies to understand their day-to-day life and its patterns.

The Aztec, Mayan, and the Inca cultures of South America had complex systems of astrology. They had around 20 zodiac signs, and these were used to study their environment. Most of the information regarding these systems is unavailable as they passed away along with their native civilizations.

The ancient Chinese too had a complex astrological system that they had developed and perfected by 1000 BCE. They named different constellations and assigned names and symbols to them. They have made a system of 24 divisions of a year, which was combined with a 28 part Moon-based zodiac. They also developed 12 branches of animal zodiacs. This ancient Chinese system is still practiced and used. They believe that all people born in a year share some come characteristics. Each year is named after an animal. For instance, 2005 was the Year of the Rooster. Like Western astrology, Chinese astrology uses elements to delineate an individual's type. So you can be a Fire Rooster or a Water Rooster as well.

Chinese astrology changed significantly when Jesuit missionaries visited and carried Western astrology to China in the 16th and 17th centuries. Nowadays, Chinese people use a far more simplified version of ancient astrology which is based on the animal year system.

The western system of zodiac too owes a lot to many different forms and branches of astrology. The Babylonians were the first to create the basic system of the zodiac. They also associated characteristics with different planets. These characters were decided by observing the planets and using metaphorical and rhetorical ideas to represent them. For instance, Mars (or Nergal for Babylonians) is red, i.e., the color of blood, and thus Mars was assigned war. Venus or Ishtar was assigned love and fertility because it appeared early in the evening like lovers. Mercury was observed to be quick and thus was assigned traits such as swiftness, agility, and deceit. This system was not created in a vacuum, and it observed many different aspects from the Middle East and the Mediterranean as well. The current names for our zodiac signs come from the Greek. The word zodiac itself is derived from 'Zoe,' which means life.

In the next chapter, we will look at the different planets in brief.

Chapter Two: Planets in Astrology

In astronomy, planets are heavenly bodies that do not have a light of their own and revolve around a star. In astrology, planets assume a different meaning than modern astronomical understanding. In the ancient times, i.e., before the invention of the telescope, the night sky was believed to be divided into two components, the fixed stars that never moved and the wandering stars that moved over the course of the year. The moving stars consisted of five planets (excluding Earth). With time the Sun and the Moon were added to the description. Thus, astrology got its classical seven planets, which are still used by modern astrologers.

For the ancients, the planets stood for the desires of the gods. These planets influenced affairs on the Earth directly. In modern times, the planets represent energies, urges, drives, etc. of the subjects.

Planets hold an important position in all forms of astrology throughout the world. They are significant in the Chinese astrology and geomancy schools as well. They also hold a crucial place in Indian astrology, where they are known as Navagraha. Let us have a look at the planets in western astrology in brief.

Classical Planets

The seven classical planets are called classical because they were known to the ancients. These planets can be seen with the naked eye. They include The Sun, The Moon, Mercury, Venus, Mars, Jupiter, and Saturn. The Sun and The Moon are sometimes also known as the 'luminaries.' Two more heavenly bodies, i.e., Vesta and Uranus, are visible to the naked eye, but no school of ancient astrology utilized them. All the classical planets are mentioned in the works of Ptolemy and Aristotle. According to these theories, all the planets have their own Celestial sphere in which they reside. These spheres are determined by their rate of speed. As the Moon is the fastest planet, it forms the first celestial sphere. All other spheres below the Moon are called sublunary spheres. The other spheres, according to the rate of speed, are Mercury, Venus, Sun, Mars, Jupiter, and finally Saturn.

The ancient astrologers described the seven classical planets in detail, and this data is still available. According to them, the planets represent basic human drives. They believed that Sun, Moon, Mercury, Venus, and Mars are personal planets while the rest were supposed to be social planets. Later Uranus, Neptune, and Pluto were added to the pantheon and ware, often known as the modern planets. Let us have a brief look at the planets, their characteristics, and their associations.

Moon

The Moon is one of the two luminaries in the field of astrology. It is considered to be the ruling planet of Cancer. It enjoys an exalted status in Taurus. According to Roman mythology, the Moon is identified either with Luna or sometimes with Diana.

The Moon is a large heavenly body that has a strong gravitational force. This force is strong enough to affect life on Earth. The Moon is responsible for the ebb and flow of the tides. Due to the Moon's revolution and rotational cycle being in sync, it revolves around the Earth in such a way that we can only see one side of the Moon all the time. The other side, which is not visible from the Earth, is known as the 'other side,' 'the dark side' or 'the far side of the Moon.'

Full Moon

The Moon guides the emotional make-up of a person. It also presides over the memories, rhythms, habits, moods, and adaptation skills of a person. It also guides how a person will react to situations and people around them. The Moon is often associated with maternal instincts, motherhood, and the home, the urge of nurturing, the past, and the need for security as well. The Moon is nostalgic about childhood and young age. She is often described as melancholic.

According to ancient medicine, the Moon is responsible for the stomach, digestive system, breasts, menstruation, and ovaries. It also presides over the pancreas. While the Moon is often described as melancholic, according to the theory of humors, it is related to the phlegmatic humor.

In modern forms of astrology, the Moon owns the fourth house while its joys are present in the third house.

The Moon's day is Monday. In fact, Monday itself was derived from Moon Day. In Romance language, Monday is known as lundi in French, luni in Romanian, lunedi in Italian, and lunes in

Spanish. All these names are derived from Luna. According to the famous Italian poet, Dante Alighieri, the Moon is related to the art of grammar.

The Moon represents the Yin life principle in Chinese astrology. Yin is the receptive and passive life principle. In Indian astrology, the Moon is known as Soma or Chandra. Here it is associated with queenship, the mind, and motherhood. In Indian astrology, the north lunar node and the south lunar node (Rahu and Ketu in Indian astrology) are considered equally important. This is why the Indian astrology consists of nine planets - the classical seven plus the lunar nodes.

Mercury

Mercury rules Gemini and Virgo both. It enjoys an exalted status in Aquarius and Virgo. In ancient Roman mythology, Mercury is supposed to be the messenger of gods thanks to his extreme speed and agility. Similarly, the planet Mercury is known for its speed as it completes its revolution around the Sun faster than any other planet. It takes only 88 days to orbit the Sun. It spends hardly 7.33 days in each zodiac sign.

Mercury is visible to the naked eye for only a short time. This is due to its proximity to the Sun. It can only be observed for a short period after the sun sets. Mercury represents a lot of things related to speed and swiftness. For instance, it guides the principles of communication, thinking, mentality, rationality, patterns, adaptability, reasoning, and variability as well.

Mercury presides over the immediate atmosphere, education, cousins and siblings, messages, forms of communication including email, telephone, etc., and physical dexterity. People who are into fields such as the internet, post, email, journalism, newspapers, writing, etc. are guided by Mercury. Mercury is often described as vivacious, inconstant, and curious.

The Planet Mercury

In ancient medicine, Mercury is supposed to rule the brain, the nervous system, the thyroid, the respiratory system, and the sensory organs. According to its position in the zodiac, Mercury is often considered to be dry and cold as compared to all the other planets.

Traditionally Mercury was supposed to have joy in the first house, but in modern astrology, it is supposed to rule the third house. It is considered to be the planet of relationships and daily expression. Mercury enjoys deconstructing things, just to reconstruct them again. It is considered to be an unemotional, curious, and opportunistic planet. Mercury's action is to take things apart and put them back together again. It is an opportunistic planet, decidedly unemotional and curious.

Venus

Venus is considered to be the ruling planet of Taurus and Libra. It is exalted in Pisces. According to Roman Mythology, Venus is supposed to be the goddess of beauty and love. She ruled passion and desire and worked with the tools of seduction. The ancient Romans adapted and adopted the myth of the Greek goddess Aphrodite for their art and literature. Venus, thus, is considered to be the Roman counterpart of Aphrodite. Venus is prominently featured in art, literature, music, and many other art forms.

Venus (the planet) completes its revolution around the Sun in 225 days. It spends around 18.75 days in each zodiac sign. Venus is often called the morning star (and in some cases the evening star) because it is the second-brightest object in the night sky, surpassed only by the Moon. Venus is known as the twin planet of Earth.

According to astrology, Venus stands for the principles of harmony, beauty, resilience, solidarity, refinement, equality, and affections. It also represents the urge to sympathize and help others. Venus is heavily involved in the desire for comfort, ease, calm, and pleasure. Venus is the ruling planet for all types of relationships, including romantic relationships, sexual relationships, marriage, and even business partnerships. Venus also presides over the arts, sex, social life, and fashion. Venus is known for her generosity and pleasant nature.

The Planet Venus

In traditional medicine, the planet Venus is thought to be related to the veins, the lumbar region, the throat, the kidneys, and the parathyroid. Venus is considered to be moist and slightly warm. As per the theory of humors, Venus is associated with the phlegmatic humor.

According to modern astrology, Venus is considered to be the ruler of the seventh house.

Venus is associated with Friday, and it is no wonder that in many languages derived from Latin, the word Venus is often similar to the word for Friday. This is seen in languages such as Spanish, Romanian, Italian, and French. The famous Italian writer Dante Alighieri believed that Venus ruled the art rhetoric.

In traditional Chinese astrology, Venus is related to the metal element. According to this, Venus is persistent, unyielding, and strong. In Indian astrology, Venus is known as Shukra. Even in Indian philosophy and astrology. Shukra, i.e., Venus stands for pleasure, wealth, and the reproductive system.

Sun

The Sun is the second luminary in the field of astrology. It is considered to be the ruler of Leo and enjoys an exalted status in Aries. In Roman mythology, the Sun was represented by Sol, which was later changed to Apollo, the god of light. In Greek mythology, the Sun is represented by two Titans - Helios and Hyperion.

The Sun enjoys a crucial place in our solar system, as it is the only star in our system around while all the planets revolve. It is crucial for life, heat, and light. The Sun travels in an arc throughout the year, which is actually the orbit of Earth around the Sun. This arc is larger around the north and south while shorter near the equator. This is why we have different day and night times and seasons throughout the year.

The Sun travels through all the twelve zodiac signs throughout the year and spends around a month in each sign. As it stays for around a month in every sign, the Sun's position on a person's birthday is used to determine his or her sun sign. The Sun sign, however, changes according to the school of astrology; for instance, in Hindu astrology, the sign change happens around the 14-15 of every month while in Western astrology, it changes around the 22-23 of each month. This change happens due to the varied system of planetary calculations. The Indian or Hindu astrology follows the sidereal definition of calculation while the Western form follows the tropical calculation.

The Sun as star (planet)

According to astrology, the Sun is believed to represent an expression of the conscious ego. It also guides the self, pride, personal power, authority, and leadership qualities. It also presides over health and vitality, creativity, life force, and spontaneity.

The Sun has been worshiped as a divine figure or god since time in memoriam. It finds an important place in many ancient as well as modern religions and cultures. One of the earliest recorded references to the divine status of the Sun is from Epic of Gilgamesh. The Sun is considered to be favorable and benign.

In traditional medicine, the Sun guides the circulatory system, the heart, and the thymus. It is also responsible for the crucial Vitamin D. Vitamin D is essential for the immune system and health of bones. In Ayurveda (the school of ancient Indian medicine), the Sun is responsible for 'Prana Shakti' or life force. It controls the stomach, bile, eyes, and bones.

In modern astrology, the Sun governs the fifth house, but according to traditional astrology, its joy resides in the ninth house.

The Sun is related to Sunday. According to the Italian poet, Dante Alighieri, the Sun guides the art of music. In Chinese astrology, the Sun is the manifestation of the Yang life principle. It is masculine, assertive, and active.

Mars

Mars governs the signs of Scorpio and Aries. It enjoys an exalted status in Capricorn. According to Roman mythology Mars is considered to be the god of bloodshed and war. He is represented with a shield and a spear.

The planet Mars and human blood both contain a lot of iron, which gives them their distinct color. Mars, the Roman god, enjoys a prominent place in the Roman pantheon where he is often placed after Jupiter and Saturn. He was worshiped by all Roman legions.

Mars takes 687 days to complete one single revolution around the Earth. It spends around 57.25 days in each zodiac sign. Mars is the first planet that is present outside the orbit of the Earth, and thus it does not set with the Sun. Mars has two polar ice caps. It rains dry ice on the surface of Mars.

According to astrology, Mars guides the principles of self-assertion, confidence, sexuality, aggression, ambition, strength, energy, and impulsiveness. It presides over competitions, sports, and all other physical activities. People have described Mars as lesser malefic and ardent.

In the field of medicine, Mars rules the muscular system, the genitals, adrenal glands, and the gonads. According to the theory of humors, Mars rules the choleric humor. It is considered to be excessively dry, hot, and sometimes rough. It was generally associated with trauma, fever, pain, accidents, and surgery, among many other things.

The Planet Mars

According to traditional astrology, Mars governs third and tenth houses while its joy is present in the sixth house, but as per modern astrology, Mars is the primary ruler of the first house. Venus controls the overall environment of any relationship, but Mars controls the action, the impulse, the discipline, and the stamina in a relationship. It also controls the masculine aspect and willpower.

Tuesday is traditionally considered to be the day of Mars. In all Roman languages, the word for Tuesday is based on Mars. For instance, in Spanish it is Martes, in Romanian it is Marti, in Italian it is martedi, and in French it is mardi. Even the English word has been taken from 'Tyr's Day.' Tyr is the Germanic form of Mars.

According to Dante, Mars governs the liberal arts of arithmetic.

In Chinese astrology, Mars is governed by the element of fire. This makes it passionate, adventurous, and energetic. In Indian (Hindu) astrology, Mars is known as Mangala and is concerned with confidence, energy, and ego.

Jupiter

Jupiter rules Pisces and Sagittarius while it enjoys an exalted status in Caner. According to classical Roman mythology, Jupiter is considered to be the king of gods who is responsible for protecting and guiding them. He is represented with a thunderbolt. Jupiter's Greek counterpart is Zeus. According to the ancient Romans, Jupiter blessed them with supremacy because they honored and worshiped him more than any other people. Jupiter guided internal organizations, external relations, and also was the divine authority in all of Rome's highest offices.

Jupiter, the planet, enjoys a similar position in the solar system. It is considered to be the king of all the planets thanks to its size. It has intensely colored clouds and all-round stormy weather. According to many astronomers,

Jupiter holds an important place in the solar system because it has an impressive gravitational force. This gravitational force captures a lot of asteroids and other space debris that otherwise would have hit the Earth and other inner planets. Jupiter takes a long time to revolve around the Sun. The orbit is around 11.9 years. It spends about a year (361) days in each zodiac sign. Jupiter is normally the fourth brightest object in the sky after the Sun, the Moon, and Venus.

Jupiter is considered quite important, according to astrology. It is related to expansion, principles of growth, good fortune, prosperity, etc. Jupiter also presides over higher education, long-distance travel, wealth, big business, religion, higher education, law, and many others. It is also related to exploration and freedom. Another aspect that Jupiter is related to is gambling and enjoyment.

Jupiter is described as benign, temperate, and greater benefic. It is considered to be moist and warm in nature, which makes it favorable to life.

In medicine, Jupiter is often associated with the pituitary gland, the liver, and fats. According to the theory of humors, Jupiter governs over sanguine humor. In traditional astrology, Jupiter ruled over the ninth and the second house, but in modern astrology, Jupiter is considered to be the primary ruler of the ninth house. According to traditional astrology, Jupiter had its joy in the eleventh house, which is traditionally associated with good luck.

Thursday is considered to be the day of Jupiter. Like other planets, the word for Thursday in Romance language is derived from Jupiter. For instance, in French it is jeudi, in Romanian it is joi, in Spanish it is jueves, and in Italian it is giovedi. According to Dante, Jupiter rules over the art of geometry.

According to Chinese astrology, the element of wood rules Jupiter, which makes it hard working, patient, and reliable. In Indian astrology, Jupiter is either known as Guru or Brihaspati. It is known as the great teacher in Sanskrit.

Saturn

Saturn rules over Aquarius and Capricorn and enjoys an exalted status in Libra. In Roman mythology, Saturn is supposed to be the god of agriculture, seeds, harvest, crops, and other related things. He is also the father of civilization and the leader of Titans. He also formed social orders and presided over conformity. Saturn is the Roman counterpart of the Greek Titan Cronus, which makes him the ruler of time as well. Saturn's symbol is known as the "crescent below the cross." It is similar to Jupiter's symbol; however, Jupiter's symbol is known as "crescent above the cross."

Saturn is well known for the rings that enclose it. It is also the second-largest planet in the solar system. The rings around the planet are supposed to represent the limits of human beings. Saturn takes around 29.5 years to complete one revolution around the Sun. It spends around 2.46 years in each zodiac sign.

In ancient Roman culture, Saturn was supposed to be the most important of all the gods, a position that he shared with Jupiter. Saturn was also supposed to be extremely powerful.

In an astrological sense, Saturn is related to precision, focus, nobility, civility, ethics, career, big goals, big achievements, authority and authority figures, dedication, hierarchy, virtues, stability, lessons, productiveness, karma, traditions, protective roles, structures, and balance. While Saturn is related to a lot of positive ideas, it is also related to many negative and neutral ones, as well. These include anxiety, restrictions, boundaries, limitations, tests, reality, practicality, and time. It presides over the sense of commitment, duty, responsibility, and mental and physical endurance in the time of crisis. Saturn is also related to foresight and planning. As Saturn takes a long time to come back to a zodiac sign, its return is supposed to bring a lot of significant changes in a person's life. Saturn is often thought to be morose, sad, and greater malefic.

According to the ancient medicine and theorist Claudius Ptolemy, Saturn governs the spleen, the right ear, the phlegm, the bladder, and the bones. Saturn is related to cold and dry things and situations. These things are necessary as they keep the balance of life well maintained. According to the theory of humors, Saturn governs melancholic humor.

The Planet Saturn

Before the planet Uranus was discovered officially, Saturn was supposed to rule Aquarius along with Capricorn.

Even today, many traditional astrologers consider Saturn to be the governor of Aquarius and Capricorn both. In tradition astrology, Saturn was supposed to rule the first and the eight houses while its joy lay in the twelfth house, which represents bad luck and mischief. Modern astrologers consider Saturn to the native ruler of the tenth house.

Saturday is associated with Saturn. It was named directly after Saturn. According to Dante, Saturn presides over the art of Astronomia, i.e., astrology and astronomy.

In Chinese astrology, the element earth governs Saturn. It makes it generous, warm, and cooperative. In Hindu or Indian astrology, Saturn is known as Shani. He is considered to bring negativity, hardships, problems, and obstacles in the life of a person.

All the above planets are considered to be the classical seven planets. Modern astrology uses more than seven planets. These planets are known as modern planets. Let us have a brief look at them.

Modern Planets

After the telescope was invented and new planets were discovered, Western astrology quickly added these planets to its pantheon. The

Indian and Chinese, however, stuck to their original seven-planet systems. Modern astrologers sat down and associated characteristics, methods, meanings, etc. to the newly discovered planets often by comparing events of global importance and significance. As these planets were added into the Western system by Western astrologers, and most of the events that they considered for the above procedure were predominantly west centric as well. According to the astrologers, these new planets are considered to be 'extra-Saturnian.' They are generational planets and are 'impersonal.' This means they don't have a significant influence on individuals, rather their influence is seen on the whole generations. They only show strong influence in an individual's life when they feature predominantly in their birth-chart. Let us now have a brief look at these planets one by one.

Uranus

Uranus is the first modern planet, and it is considered to be the ruler of Aquarius. It enjoys an exalted status in Scorpio. In ancient Greek mythology, Uranus is supposed to be the personification of the sky itself. Uranus, the planet, is extremely unusual as compared to all other planets because it rotates on its sides. Due to this, it presents all of its poles to the Sun alternatively. This means its hemispheres alternate between being soaked in light and lying in total darkness throughout its orbit.

Uranus has a long period of revolution and takes 84 years to complete one orbit. It spends around seven years in each zodiac sign. It was first discovered and accepted as a planet by Sir William Herschel in the year 1781.

According to astrology, Uranus governs unconventional and new ideas, ingenuity, electricity, discoveries, individuality, inventions, revolutions, and democracy. It also governs genius more than any other planets.

The Planet Uranus

Uranus presides over clubs, societies, and all groups that are based on progressive ideas and humanitarian principles. Uranus is sudden; it governs freedom, sudden changes, and originality. It is also the ruling planet of revolutionary and radical ideas.

Uranus is traditionally associated with Wednesday, along with Mercury.

The discovery of Uranus happened around the time of the rise of Romanticism in arts and literature. This is why Uranus is considered to be the ruling planet of creative expression, individuality, and freedom.

In the field of medicine, Uranus is generally associated with mental disorders, the sympathetic nervous system, hysteria, breakdowns, cramps, and spasms. According to contemporary astrologers, Uranus is the ruler of the eleventh house.

Neptune

Neptune is considered to be the ruler of Pisces and enjoys an exalted status in Leo. In Roman mythology, Neptune was supposed to be the god of oceans and seas. The planet Neptune is a deep, blue color, which justifies the symbolism. Neptune's symbol is a trident, a weapon traditionally associated with Neptune. Neptune takes 165 years to complete one revolution around the Sun. It spends around 14 years in each zodiac sign. Neptune was first identified in the year 1846.

The Planet Neptune

According to astrology, Neptune is the planet of dreams, idealism, dissolution, extremities, empathy, and artistry. It is also the planet of vagueness and illusion. Along with Venus, Neptune is associated with Friday, as well. This is due to Neptune's place, which is in the higher octave of Venus. When Neptune was discovered, the arts started becoming subtler and start moving away from literal representations.

In the field of medicine, Neptune is related to the spinal canal, the thalamus, neuroses, and uncertain illnesses. According to modern astrologers, Neptune is the ruling god of the twelfth house.

Pluto

Pluto is one of the most debated heavenly bodies. It is the ruling planet of Scorpio and enjoys the exalted status in Virgo according to modern astrology. In Roman mythology, Pluto is supposed to be the god of the underworld. He is supposed to be extremely rich. When Pluto was discovered, it was allotted the alchemy symbol.

Pluto takes around 248 years to complete a full circle of the zodiac, but its progress fluctuates throughout this circuit. It can spend anywhere between 15 to 26 years in each zodiac sign.

According to astrology, Pluto is known as the great renewer because it represents destruction for renewal. It is like the phoenix that rises from the ashes. One of the most used words to describe Pluto is transformation. It is often associated with personal mastery, power, sharing, and cooperation. Pluto is the ruler of mining, extreme wealth, detective work, espionage, surgery, business, and all industries that are related to mining and digging. Along with Mars, Pluto is also associated with Tuesday.

Pluto was first discovered in 1930; however, it had started displaying effects from 1914 itself when it entered Cancer. Its entry in Cancer marks the beginning of World War I. In the 1930s, its discovery was associated with nuclear research, the Cold War, and the rise of consumerism and crony capitalism. The discovery of Pluto is also marked by the beginning of modern psychoanalysis as the pioneers in the field, Freud and Jung both delved deep into the human psyche around these years.

Pluto has played an important role as it is believed that it influenced many major art schools and movements. Surrealism and

Cubism, both deconstructionist movements of arts, are said to be inspired by Pluto. In medicine, Pluto is associated with regenerative forces, reproductive system, cell formation, etc. Pluto is not considered to be a ruling planet by traditional astrologers, but they often utilize it for predictive work. In modern astrology, Pluto is considered to be the ruler of the eighth house.

Ceres

Ceres is considered to be the smallest dwarf planet in the solar system, which has been identified by now, but it is the largest object in the asteroid belt. Giuseppe Piazzi discovered this dwarf planet in 1801. It is named after the Roman goddess Ceres. Ceres is the goddess of the harvest, growing plants, and motherly love. It was the first asteroid to be ever discovered, and it takes around one-third mass of the entire asteroid belt. The classification of Ceres has been quite controversial, and it has been changed multiple times. Johann Elert Bode believed it to be the missing planet that he believed existed between Mars and Jupiter. Ceres was quickly assigned a planetary symbol and was considered a planet for at least five decades. In the year 2006, a debate arose regarding the status of Pluto, and once again, plans of making Ceres a planet were discussed. Ultimately Pluto and Ceres both became dwarf planets, a newly formulated category.

Ceres takes around four years and seven months to pass through all the zodiac signs. It resides in each zodiac for about two years and six months. Ceres is considered to be the Roman equivalent of the Greek goddess Demeter. Demeter is traditionally associated with agriculture. The planet and the goddess both are related to fertility, pregnancy, and female problems. They also govern significant transitions in women's lives. These include family bonds, gestation periods, relationships, etc. According to traditional astrologers, Ceres is considered to be the ruler of Virgo, but modern astrologers consider her to be the ruler of Taurus. Ceres still enjoys an exalted status in Virgo. Chiron also rules Taurus according to certain modern astrologers. Chiron is also supposed to rule Virgo and enjoys an exalted position in Sagittarius.

While Ceres governs mothers and motherhood, she is still considered to be a virgin goddess.

Ceres governs independent and unmarried women, as according to her myth, Ceres, an unmarried goddess, became a mother without the help of a husband. The Moon represents ideal motherhood, while Ceres represents natural and real motherhood.

Ceres (Dwarf planet)

Ceres is a goddess who controls natural cycles and resources. According to astrology, Ceres is considered to be the ruling planet of the environment. According to mythology, Erysichthon molested Earth and cut down trees in a grove, which was sacred to Demeter and Ceres. He was punished for this act by the gods and was cursed with fearful hunger. In the 21st century, Ceres has assumed a special place in the environmental movement. It also governs communal harmony and social activism.

As it is clear that current definitions of planets vary a lot in astrology and astronomy. In astrology, planets include all celestial bodies while astronomy believes that there are only eight planets in our solar system. Regardless, planets and celestial bodies play an integral part in the zodiac and all branches of astrology. Without studying planets, it is impossible to make predictions and understand the personality of an individual. But understanding the planets and their characteristics is just the half deal. Planets, their position in the birth-chart, and their relations with each other need to be studied in detail to understand a person thoroughly. The next chapter will tackle this problem.

Chapter Three: Birth Charts and Houses

In the last chapter, we saw different planets and their relevance to astrology. But mere planets cannot help you understand your personality, the position of planets in your birth chart, and their relations with each other define your characteristics.

Everyone who loves astrology and wants to understand it seriously should study birth charts. While horoscopes are great for beginners, they are incomplete and sometimes incorrect. They should serve as a starting point, after which you need to delve deeper into the ocean of zodiac and astrology.

All the planets and asteroids are placed within a house. These positions are crucial because they offer a lot of information regarding the individual, their personality, their relationship with the world, and how they act in day-to-day life as well. Houses are, in a way, the map to your past, present, and future. The planets move through these houses and bring in significant physical as well as emotional changes in your life and personality.

Without Houses and birth charts, astrology is incomplete. The Houses make astrology so perfect and on the point. Each House signifies a certain component of our day-to-day life, whether physical, social, or emotional. But these houses do not work in a vacuum, and they work together as a unit. It is made up of a complete 360-degree wheel.

To calculate your birth chart, either visit a trustworthy astrologer or use a free web-service. Both these services can help you create the perfect birth chart. Avoid paying too much for the birth chart as it is just the map of your life (unless they include a proper and total reading as well.)

What are the Houses?

Each birth chart is divided into twelve equal parts. Each of these parts represents a House. The number twelve is used quite often in astrology, as it is a perfect number. Houses should not be confused with the zodiac wheel. A zodiac wheel is based on the Sun's annual rotational movement, while the House system is based on the Earth's daylong rotational system.

When reading a birth chart, astrologers combine these two to achieve accurate readings.

The Houses are constantly moving and move around every 24 hours. It is, therefore, crucial to enter your exact birth time while making a birth chart. The Houses shift every four minutes, so individuals born on the very same day may have drastically different birth charts.

The House reflects a lot of things about your personality and life. By understanding them thoroughly, you can understand your position in life and how you can use your talents to overcome obstacles, if any. If your birth time is inaccurate, your birth chart will be inaccurate as well, which may lead to inaccurate or faulty readings.

The Language of the Houses

When you look at a birth chart for the first time, you may find it confusing and daunting. Certain areas of birth charts may be full of writings and symbols, while others might be totally blank. You may be confused about the directions and the meaning of those symbols as well.

Reading charts is not difficult, and you can do it with no efforts if you know the basics. To start reading a birth chart, you first need to know the Ascendant. The Ascendant or the rising sign is the leftmost point of the central horizon line. It depicts the zodiac sign that was rising from the eastern horizon at the time of your birth. The Sun sign reveals the truth about our outer personality, while the moon sign reveals our emotions. The Ascendant, however, depicts our personal landscape and how you will act in your life. For instance, a person with Aquarius ascendant will be unique and a revolutionary while a Gemini ascendant will be loquacious and talkative. You will find more about ascendants later in this book.

The Ascendant also helps you find out the ruling planet of your chart. For instance, a person with Pisces ascendant will be ruled by Neptune while a person born under a Sagittarius ascendant will be ruled by Jupiter.

The Ascendant is also used to understand the birth chart. Birth charts are read counterclockwise. The horizontal line of the Ascendant is the first House of the chart. Moving along the right side of the first House, you will get all the twelve houses. The twelfth House will border the rising sign towards the north.

Once you understand the signs and planets, you can move on to Houses to understand their energies and what they are trying to do in your life.

While analyzing your birth chart, it is possible that you may have more than one planet in one house, and others might be totally empty as well. Do not worry about this; it is perfectly normal. Only the locations of the planets matter, and empty houses can be safely ignored.

Interpreting the Houses in Your Own Birth Chart

The Ascendant is like an anchor. Once you set it up, you can easily identify other houses and the planets present in them. Each planet has a specific function; for instance, Venus is concerned with love life; Mercury is concerned with communications, etc. Each of these planets may act differently according to their sign. Mercury in Capricorn will be loquacious yet serious. They will know how to communicate in a rational and logical manner. Similarly, a strong Venus in Scorpio will make romances and life mysterious and exciting. Contrasting planets and signs can lead to interesting combinations. For instance, if Mars is a strong presence in Cancer, then Cancers may become passive-aggressive and grumpy.

Once both the signs and planets have been understood, you need to understand their roles, their compatibility, and how can they help you.

Our birth charts are constant, and they cannot change, as they are literally the snapshots of the position of the stars at the time of our birth. While the birth chart remains stationary, the planet continues to move in the sky. Planets continuously move around houses and create new challenges and situations.

Now that the basics of Houses and birth charts are clear, let us have a look at the 12 Houses one by one.

Astrological Houses

The 1st House

The First House is also known as the House of the Ascendant. It represents the body that you are born with. It reflects your general temperament, along with your physical appearance. People born with any natal planet that is present in this House will have a significant influence on the individual's life. For instance, if you were born with Mercury in the First house, then you will be loquacious; if you were born with the Moon in the First House, then you will be emotional and will be in touch with your feelings. This is the first stop for transiting planets. It represents goals, new projects, ideas, a new perspective, and similar things. This House is governed by Aries.

The 2nd House

The Second House is associated with material possessions, personal finances, and the overall materialistic world. People born with natal planets in this House often try to find a sense of security in the material world. Planets transiting through this House often introduce changes in self-esteem. This House is governed by Taurus.

The 3rd House

This House is closely associated with the local community, communication, and transportation. People born with natal planets in this House are often trying to build good relationships with their partners, friends, coworkers, siblings, classmates, etc. They love expressiveness. When planets are moving through this House, people may receive important information about others. This House is governed by Gemini.

The 4th House

The Fourth House is situated at the base of the birth chart. It is associated with family and home. It is also associated with a person's relationship with their mother or maternal figure. It is also related to domesticity and family matters. Transiting planets through this House often encourage people to invest in infrastructure. They also enable people to create more nurturing places and spaces. This House is related to Cancer.

The 5th House

This House is related to romance, creativity, and children. People born with natal planets in this House are known to be artistic, creative, and imaginative. Planets transiting through this House often lead to 'Eureka' moments. It is also linked to sudden confidence boosts. This House is ruled by Leo.

The 6th House

The Sixth House is associated with wellness, health, and day-to-day routines. It is also associated with odd jobs and chores. While the First House represents the body that you are born with, the Sixth House represents the body that you achieve throughout your life. People with natal planets in this House love to be practical, organized, and structured. They like to focus on things such as calendar and time management. They love to create schedules and follow them, as well. This House is ruled by Virgo.

The 7th House

The Seventh House is also known as the Descendent. It sits right opposite the First House Ascendant. All the houses until now are associated with the physical and material world as they represent money, friends, domesticity, etc. From the Seventh House onwards, the Houses start looking deep into the individuals themselves. Seventh House represents your cosmic mind, and it governs your relationships. People with natal planets in this House are often focused on relationships and try to find good partners in almost all aspects of their life. Planets transiting through this House can help you close deals and make concrete bonds with others. This House is ruled by Libra.

The 8th House

The Eighth House is associated with a lot of 'different' (for the lack of better term) things. It is associated with death, sex, and transformation. Some astrologers like to call it the 'haunted house' thanks to its 'negative' associations. People with natal planets in this House are often attracted to paranormal, supernatural, occult, and similar topics. They often have passionate romances and relationships. Planets moving through this House can help you understand the core of things and can help you remember the complexities of life. This House is governed by Scorpio.

The 9th House

This House is associated with higher education, philosophy, and travel. In medieval astrology, this House was associated with locations and people outside your town. Now, this House stands for intellectual exploration. People with natal planets in this House are extremely curious. They have wanderlust and are inquisitive. When planets transit through this House, people often tend to study new things. They can even adopt totally diametrical perspectives of things. Some people often leave their current place and move out to other countries. This House is governed by Sagittarius.

The 10th House

The Tenth House occupies the topmost position in the birth chart. It is the apex of your individual story. The Midheaven, which is the highest point in your birth chart, is placed in the Tenth House (often) and represents the zenith of your success. This House represents your professional aspirations, your public image, and your achievements in your professional life. Natal Planets in the Tenth House are a sign of an ambitious person. When planets transit through House, people tend to change careers. This House is governed by Capricorn.

The 11th House

This House reminds everyone of hard work and effort. It is associated with humanitarian projects and distant things. Innovation and technology too is governed by this House. People who are born with planets in this House are technologically oriented. They often come up with challenging and revolutionary ideas. Transiting planets through this House can help you define your role in society. This House is ruled by Aquarius.

The 12th House

The twelfth House is positioned just below the horizon in the sky. It thus depicts the darkness before the dawn. It represents 'unseen and unknown' realms. It governs everything that does not have a physical form, including secrets, dreams, feelings, and emotions. People who have planets in this House are intuitive and smart. Some of them can even be psychics. When planets transit through this House, people tend to attract one another a lot. It should be remembered that not all relationships can last long, and some of them must come to an end. This House represents Pisces.

Chapter Four: The Twelve Signs

According to the Western astrology system, twelve astrological or zodiac signs are divided into twelve sectors of the ecliptic. Each of these sectors is 30°. They begin at the vernal equinox, which is one of the many intersections of the ecliptic with the celestial equator. This position is also known as the First Point of Aries. This why Aries is considered to be the first sign of the zodiac, which is followed by Taurus, Gemini, Cancer, Leo, Virgo, Libra, Scorpio, Sagittarius, Capricorn, Aquarius, and Pisces. Each of these sectors has its constellations, after which they have been named.

The concept of the zodiac is ancient. It first began in the Babylonian astrology system. It was later modified and adapted according to the Hellenistic society. Astrology says that all celestial phenomena affect human activity. The signs follow the paths of the stars. While there has been some research in the past that have 'debunked' astrology, believers still exist. Science has been wrong a lot of times, and believers believe that we still do not have the capabilities and technology to understand astrology yet.

Scientists may call it pseudoscience, but astrology, if done properly, can work.

People have used many different styles and methods of measuring and dividing the sky into various parts. Yet, the names of the zodiacs and symbols remain constant. For instance, Western astrology measures the parts from Equinox and Solstice. Indian astrology, also known as Vedic or Hindu astrology, measures these parts using the equatorial plane method.

In Western and Vedic astrology, space and the movement of planets, including the Sun and the Moon, matters a lot. These planets move through the zodiac signs. In the Chinese system, instead of space, time is emphasized. The Chinese system focuses on the hours, months, and the years and their cycles.

Sun Signs

The Sun is the most important object in our solar system because of it responsible for our lives. Without the Sun, life would not have existed. The Sun is at the center of our solar system, and all the planets revolve around it. It is a huge ball of energy that powers our lives. But along with giving us life, it also affects it significantly. As the Sun is the largest object in our solar system, it plays an integral role in astrology. The Sun is related to your physical shape, your exterior image, and your notion of physical self as well. On the other hand, your emotional makeup is handled by the Moon, which will be discussed later. The Sun is related to confidence, the present, and ambition. While other planets affect your life significantly, the Sun affects it the most.

The Sun is the ultimate ruler of the zodiac. The Sun is different than any other planet. For instance, the Sun affects the creative life forces while Mars controls raw strength and energy. Astrologers often say that Mars is action, and the Sun is the reaction. Mars can often cause you to take mindless decisions, while the Sun will encourage you to be smart and tactful. Thus, the Sun is rightfully known as the king of the birth chart. It provides us life force and the will to live. It keeps our soul fresh, active, and lit. The position of the Sun in the skies at the time of a person's birth is crucial. The position of the Sun at the time of your birth determines your Sun Sign. For instance, if at the time of your birth, the Sun was traveling through Cancer, then your sun sign will be Cancer. While the birth chart is necessary to understand your fate and life, you can use the Sun sign to understand how you carry yourself in your life quickly. Your Sun sign controls your personality and displays it to the world in its full glory.

Locating Sun sign on a birth chart is easy. We know that the Sun does not move and it is the Earth that rotates and revolves continuously, however, for the sake of astrology, it is assumed that the Sun travels through twelve zodiac signs throughout the year. Sun sings your nature, your attitude towards life, and your personality. These things are permanent. Your personality does not change according to age, your situation, or time. Sun sign also reflects your power and strength. For instance, people born under Cancer sun sigs are often family-oriented and enjoy the domesticity of life. These people do best in homes and related situations. People born under the Sagittarius sun sign love new adventures and foreign places. Similarly, Aquarius loves being an iconoclast.

The Sun also reflects your ego and what things you love. Your motivation is reflected in your sun sign, as well. Whatever your motivation, each sun sign will do it differently. This is why no person is alike. The Sun sign, along with many different aspects of astrology, makes us unique individuals. Knowing your sun sign is like knowing the tip of the iceberg. If you want to find out more about yourself, you need to understand and focus on many other aspects of astrology, as well. But for beginners, and for people who are short on time, sun sign can help you get some crucial hints about a person's personality and behavior.

Aries

Aries is the first sign of the zodiac. It is well known for its pioneering instinct and upbeat nature. Aries is ruled by the element of fire, and thus it loves to live in the movement and loves to be furious, fast, swift, and on its toes. They are natural leaders, and you may find it impossible to ignore them. They love to take on challenges and love to be in charge. Aries are highly competitive and courageous. They do not like traveling on the oft-trodden paths; rather, they love to create their ways. It is a fearless sign that is passionate, warrior-like, and has tremendous ardor.

Positive Traits

Aries is fearless, courageous, and bold. They love to take charge and are born-leaders. They love to succeed and work hard for it.

Negative traits

Aries can be brazen and can make haphazard decisions. They can be inconsiderate of people who are in the path of their success. Some Aries can be uncaring, bossy, and pushy.

Advice

Aries should try to avoid being too fiery and impulsive. While their fieriness and impulsive nature set them apart, too much of these things can make Aries unpopular among friends, family, and colleagues. Instead of making haphazard decisions and landing in trouble, Aries should learn how to slow down and should think twice before acting.

Celebrities

Some well know Arians are Emma Watson, Lady Gaga, James Franco, Robert Downey Jr., Reese Witherspoon, Seth Rogen, Quentin Tarantino, etc.

Tarot Card: The Emperor

The Tarot card for Aries is The Emperor. The Emperor represents Aries thoroughly. It is a natural leader, just like Aries. The Emperor also represents loyalty and the ability to maintain courage and posture through calm and calamity.

Aries uses a sense of authority to help their friends. It also represents Aries's goal-oriented attitude.

Symbol: Ram's Head

Aries is associated with the Ram. Its symbol consists of the horns and face of the Ram. The Ram is a regal animal that is known to be confident, bold, and brave. It charges at its opponents, just like the Aries charges at opportunities. It represents Aries's tendency to make its path. The Ram also represents initiative, action, courage, and authority.

Ruling Planet: Mars

Like other symbols and objects related to Aries, its ruling planet too is well known for being headstrong and courageous. Mars is the Roman god of warriors and war, and similarly, Ares is the Greek god of war. Mars, the planet, represents aggression, action, and drive. It represents Aries's quality of influencing others and enhances their energy to do so. Mars is considered to be a pioneer like its counterpart.

Ruling House: 1st House of Self

Aries rules the 1st house. This house represents your total self. This includes your attitude, personality, traits, etc. that make up your personality. Aries represents creativity, self-drive, and identity- all these traits are present in the first house.

Element: Fire

As said earlier, Aries is ruled by the element of fire. Fire fuels Aries's various traits, including desire, passion, and courage. Fire is high-spirited and high-spirited. It cannot be controlled or trapped. Aries can often be like volcanoes; they can suddenly burst without warning and show immense aggression and joy. The element of fire is present in all the activities that an Aries undertakes.

Color: Red

As said earlier, Mars is the ruling planet of Aries. Mars is also known as the Red planet, so it should not come as a surprise that Aries's representative color is red. Red is known to be the color of desire, passion, danger, and excitement. This, combined with fire's eagerness and energy, makes Aries a strong-willed person. Red is extremely vibrant, and it is difficult to ignore it, just as it is difficult to ignore or avoid Aries. Aries are recommended to surround themselves with the color red as it can enhance their natural characteristics.

Quality: Cardinal

Aries is a cardinal sign and is also the pioneering sign. The Sun moves into Aries at the beginning of every astrological year. It enters the sign around the time of Spring Equinox, which makes the atmosphere quite pleasant. Cardinal signs are considered to be 'starter,' i.e., they understand how to start things and are well-rounded initiators. Their energy and passion for their life make Aries highly confident and high-spirited.

Gemini

Gemini is a smart, curious, and clever sign that is not only full of ideas but can communicate them well as well. Geminis are known for their quick thinking prowess. They are extremely versatile and possess immense adaptability. They are often thought to have a split personality, which is represented by their symbol- The Twins. They are highly intelligent but scatterbrained as well. They love talking with others and sharing their knowledge and information. They are like sponges who love to absorb everything that is around them. Gemini is always thirsty for new things and knowledge. They are also known to be very talkative. They love to socialize and always try to have a good time. They love variety, which is why they are often considered to be unpredictable.

Positive Traits

Geminis are extremely versatile, and they can jump from one topic to another without any lags or problems. It is great to have them around, as they will keep you on your toes all the time.

Negative Traits

Geminis are restless, and sitting still or listening to others patiently is not their cup of tea. They are easily distracted and thus jump from task to task without finishing the one at hand as well.

Advice

Avoid jumping off topics all the time. To do this, the best option is to try to relax and calm your mind. Their many methods for calming your mind, some of the most common ones include breathing exercises, yoga, mindfulness practice, meditation, etc. If you are able to slow down, you will be able to finish your tasks on time as well.

Gemini celebrities

There are many world-renowned celebrities who were born under the Gemini sign. These include Johnny Depp, Angelina Jolie, Marilyn Monroe, Nicole Kidman, Liam Neeson, Mark Wahlberg, Neil Patrick Harris, Prince William, and Colin Farrell.

Tarot Card: The Lovers

The Tarot card for Gemini is similar to its symbol- it involves two people. The Tarot card for Gemini is The Lovers. The Lovers card represents marriage, love, unity, and union. In simpler words, The Lovers card represents the union of two people to become one single entity. Like its sign, Gemini is famous for having two opposite personalities living together in one body. This is represented well by its Tarot card. Similarly, Geminis are known to perform well when other people are involved or present. This idea of involving other people once again shows the importance of union for Geminis.

Symbol: The Twins

The symbol of Gemini, as said earlier, is the Twins. Its glyph is represented with the Roman numeral for 2 (II). These two pillars represent how there are at least two sides to the character of all people. As Geminis often have two or more sides, they are easily adaptable and can form friendships and new relationships with ease as well.

Planet: Mercury

Mercury is the ruling planet of Gemini. Mercury is known as the planet of communication as, according to Roman mythology, Mercury was supposed to be the messenger of Gods. Mercury guides the channel through which we communicate. Gemini absorbs a lot of knowledge and information, and Mercury encourages it to share it with the world. This knowledge is often shared in the form of ideas and thoughts.

Ruling House: 3rd House of Communication

Gemini is the ruler of the 3rd house, as it is the third sign of the zodiac. The third house is the House of Communication. The position of the third house on your birth chart depicts your communication style and ideas. This house is responsible for the clarity of your thoughts, your speed of processing information, how you communicate information, etc. As Gemini is ruled by Mercury, the planet of communication, the combination of both these elements makes Gemini a chatty and communicative person. This sign is closely associated with the mind and the mouth.

Element: Air

Gemini is ruled by the element of Air as it whips up chatty storms quite often. The element of Air represents intellect and mental power. Gemini truly embraces its element because it allows the sign to multi-task. It also helps it to process information at a rapid speed and allows them to be extremely observant.

Color: Yellow

Gemini is represented by the color yellow. Yellow is an uplifting, bright, bold, and shiny color associated with life and excitement. Like the color, Geminis too are often upbeat and cheery. Like the Sun, the color yellow makes every bright and happy.

Yellow is also the color of ideas, intellect, and mind. This is reflected well in the attitude of Geminis.

Quality: Mutable

Gemini is well known for its on-the-go-demeanor and for its chatty nature. These two qualities are the reflection of their Mutable quality. Mutable signs are the ending or last signs of all the four seasons and thus reflect the change and new beginnings. Gemini can be described as a social butterfly, and it is always ready to jump from one conversation to another. It is thus no wonder that it is always ready for new beginnings and change.

Gemini represents long days and extra sunshine. These two factors are great for beginning new conversations and social interactions.

Cancer

Cancer, like its symbol, appears to be hard on the outside but is a little softy on the inside. Cancer is supposed to be one of the most sensitive signs of the zodiac. It cares for the wellbeing of others quite a lot. Cancers are famous for being loving, loyal, and tenacious. They are like the mothers of the zodiac as they will not only fiercely defend themselves, but they will also attack if anyone tries to harm their dear ones. While they are often thought to be lovers and friends, they can become vicious and downright acerbic when they see their loved ones in danger. Cancers love security, comfort, and protection; this is reflected by their symbol as well. As said earlier, Cancer is connected to motherhood as it displays the same grace and ferocity as mothers. Cancerians are highly intuitive and emotional. They are guided by their hearts and subconscious.

Positive Traits

Cancerians are protective and nurturing. They love people and taking care of them. They enjoy domesticity and can make anyone feel comfortable and loved.

Negative Traits

Cancer is an extremely sensitive sign. They often take seemingly unimportant things to heart and are bound to overreact. They are moody, and their mood can change in seconds. Many people dislike Cancer for their sudden mood swings and 'melodrama.'

Advice

Cancerians are extremely emotional and moody. Their deeply emotional nature often hurts their feelings. They are also moody and can become vicious. Cancerians can benefit a lot if they understand how to control their mood. Think before you leap is the perfect advice for Cancer.

Cancer celebrities

Some famous Cancerians are Meryl Streep, Tom Hanks, Will Ferrell, Ariana Grande, Princess Diana, Tom Cruise, Chris Pratt, Sofia Vergara, Selena Gomez, Kathy Bates, Robin Williams, and Liv Tyler.

Tarot Card: The Chariot

The Chariot is the Tarot card of Cancer. The Chariot stands for tenacity and sensitive, which are well represented in the attitude of Cancer. Chariot encourages Cancerians to combine the power of their hearts with their heads, which will allow them to overcome the problems in their life and face the day-to-day challenges. Cancer can bring out the right reactions at the right times, just like The Chariot. The Chariot is relentless and will always take Cancerians wherever they want to go.

Symbol: The Crab

The Crab is the sign of Cancer. Its glyph depicts the crab in a simplistic form, as well. Crabs are well known for their pincers and hard shells. But their interior is luscious, soft, and sensitive. Similarly, Cancer may appear tough on the outside, but it is just an exoskeleton that protects the lovable and sensitive side underneath. Cancers love their emotions and hold them tight, just like they hold their dear ones tight. Like crabs, Cancer can become vicious and attack with their pincers if provoked.

Ruling Planet: The Moon

The Moon is considered to be the ruler of Cancer. The Moon is supposed to be emotionally driven, so it makes sense that it rules the highly intuitive and sensitive Cancer. According to astrology, the Moon controls human emotions, and Cancer is sign driven by affection, desires, and feelings. The Moon often cares for others more than themselves, which is reflected in the philosophy of Cancer as well.

Ruling House: 4th House of Security

Cancer is the fourth sign of the zodiac, and it is the ruler of the fourth house as well. The fourth house of the birth chart is the House of Security. This house guides how people relate to familiar things and brings people comfort. This house is also responsible for our memories, our family, our home, and our roots. Cancerians prioritize the feeling of homeliness and security, which is reflected well in their house as well. They prefer the safety and comfort of their homes (i.e., their shells) and avoid going out quite often. The more protected they are, the happier they will be.

Element: Water

Cancer is ruled by the element of Water. Water is known for its purity and purifying qualities, as well. It is the source of life for everyone. It acts as a sanctuary for many species. Like Water, Cancers understand how to make people feel nourished, safe, and secure. Water is an intuitive element, and Cancer is a sign ruled by intuition. Cancer uses intuition to help others by understanding what they need and desire.

Color: Silver & White

Silver and white are the colors of Cancer. These colors are known for their purity and freshness. Silver is like the shining face of the full Moon. It is also like the shiny surface of clean water. Silver is also the color of the metal silver, which is known for its purity and purifying qualities. Silver is so pure that it can even defeat evil.

Cancer is an understanding and caring sign, but it can sometimes get in trouble for being too caring, even when their intentions are innocent. Silver and white are bright colors, but they are also delicate. They can be controlled by other bold and brash colors.

Quality: Cardinal

Cancer is the harbinger of the summer season. It is a Cardinal sign. Cardinal signs are inventive and initiators. They begin things. Cancers love to bring new relationships and get new life-experiences as well. They are exceptionally capable when their emotions are at a peak. Cancer loves to help others and loves to build a family by connecting with new people. This is due to its Cardinal energy.

Leo

Leo is well known for its fun and flirtatious nature. It is also known as the most expressive signs of the zodiac. Leo is ruled by the Sun, which makes it vibrant and bold. It is ruled by the element of Fire that makes it dramatic, charming, and magnificent. Leo is always the life of the party. They love and crave attention. They always want to be the center of attraction. Leo is proud, courageous, but also kind-hearted. They are well known for being extremely loyal. They are regal and royal, just like the Lion.

As said earlier, Leos are extremely expressive, which sometimes can lead to problems. Leo love to express everything, and rarely do they hide their feelings. This often makes them seem bold and bratty. While Leos can be extremely dramatic, they are also extremely friendly and generous.

Positive Traits

Leos have a heart of gold and are full of warmth and love. They love to laugh and make others laugh, as well. Leos are extremely loyal to their loved ones.

Negative Traits

Leos are the most expressive of all the signs of the zodiac. This often makes them dramatic. They love attention and can resort to strange tactics to get this attention. They can appear arrogant and rude to some people.

Advice

Leos love glory and attention, but they should remember that others have feelings too. Leos need to learn how to be more considerate.

Leo Celebrities

Some of the well known Leos are Jennifer Lopez, Jennifer Lawrence, Mick Jagger, J.K. Rowling, Arnold Schwarzenegger, Chris Hemsworth, Mila Kunis, Leonardo DiCaprio, Madonna, Ben

Affleck, Charlize Theron, Halle Berry, Robert De Niro, etc.

Tarot Card: Strength

The Tarot card for Leo is Strength. It is an empowering card for Leo. In almost all Tarot decks, strength is represented by a figure of a lion. This shows how well connected Leo and its Tarot card are. This card is related to the most primal form of nature. It allows Leo to be in its most natural state. It not only represents physical strength, but it is also related to mental, social, heart, and soul strength. This card is also responsible for reminding Leo to balance its physical capabilities with mental abilities and emotions, including love, compassion, and generosity.

Symbol: The Lion

As the name suggests, Leo is represented by the mighty and brave lion. Its glyph is interesting because it has a dual meaning. It appears like the tail and head of a lion, but it also looks like 'lambada' or the Greek letter, which is the first letter of the word Leon or Lion. Lions are well known for their regal nature, their power, and their strength. Leo mirrors many aspects of the lion included royalty, affection, instinct, bravery, courage, and strength.

Ruling Planet: The Sun

As said earlier, Leo is ruled by the blazing and glorious Sun. The Sun is the brightest object in the solar system, and likewise, Leo tries to be the brightest person in any crowd. They always desire to be the center of attention. They do this with their personality and charm. The Sun demands attention because it is important. Similarly, Leo seeks attention, as well. The Sun can be dangerous, and similarly, Leo too can become vicious and ferocious if bothered. Its self-centered nature can sometimes be a nuisance to its loved ones and friends.

Ruling House: 5th House of Pleasure

Leo is the fifth sign of the zodiac, and it rules the 5th house of the birth chart as well. It rules the House of Pleasure. The house and its ruler both are full of energy and possess a playful and energetic spirit. The house represents creativity, fun, and expression. This house is also related to romantic life and love.

Element: Fire

Leo is governed by the element of Fire. Like Fire, it demands attention. The element of Fire keeps Leo lit, and it burns its passion for love, life, and action. Like a fire, Leo's energy and warmth light up crowds. Fire is bold and brave, just like Leo. The fire also represents Leo's confidence and strength.

Color: Gold

Regal, rich, and bright, gold defines Leo thoroughly. Since ancient times gold has been associated with power, royalty, class, and prestige. Only a select few could afford gold. So, it is no wonder that Leo is represented by the color gold. This expressive and expensive shade catches everyone's attention without any effort. It can be so bright that it may even blind you. Gold is pompous and flamboyant, just like Leo. It is also associated with positivity, purity, and warmth, as well.

Quality: Fixed

Leo is represented by a fixed quality. It is the second sign of summer. In the scorching heat and bright light of summer, Leo lets out its rugged side and displays it with pride. Leos have immense endurance and confidence, which allows them to persevere without any problem even on the scariest days. They are optimistic and love positivity.

Virgo

The sixth sign of the zodiac is all about perfection. Virgo is extremely detail-oriented, loves working hard, and is quite critical as well. Virgo is famous for its pure yet discriminating nature. It is represented by a woman, the Virgin, to be precise. Virgo can notice flaws quickly and fix them quickly as well. They are dependable, especially if you are looking for positive (or negative) criticism. Virgos can help people reach their highest potential. One of the biggest plus points of Virgo is that they can collect a lot of information, sort it, and only keep relevant while discarding everything else quickly. This and many such habits make Virgo one of the most efficient and productive signs of all.

Positive Traits

Virgos are dependable and reliable. Virgos are always there for their friends and loved ones.

Negative Traits

Virgos are well known for their perfectionist behavior. Such behavior is great, but it can cause a lot of problems for others. It can also cause problems for Virgos themselves, as they can often act too critical.

Advice

The best advice for a Virgo would be to relax and loosen up. While a desire for perfection is great but do not let it overpower you. Nobody is perfect.

Virgo celebrities

Many superstars and talented actors are Virgos. They include Michel Jackson, Beyoncé, Blake Lively, Keanu Reeves, Jimmy Fallon, Tim Burton, Michelle Williams, Jennifer Hudson, Prince Harry, Adam Sandler, Chris Pine, Salma Hayek, Cameron Diaz, Pink, etc.

Tarot Card: The Hermit

Virgo is represented by The Hermit. The Hermit encourages Virgo to find and use quiet time and solitude to absorb, look for answers, and absorb them. Virgo is often critical and can scrutinize even the smallest details. The Hermit is the same; it takes things, mulls them over, and looks for the hidden messages. They can find the best of things, even in the trash. The Hermit also connects Virgo with spirituality and encourages them to have a meditative nature. A healthy dose of these two can keep Virgo active and confident.

Symbol: The Virgin

As said earlier, Virgo is represented by The Virgin. The Virgin is the symbol of purity and perfection. Similarly, Virgo desires perfection, which is why it can find faults almost instantaneously. Virgo understands what is right and what is wrong. Virgo and its sign both are known to be supportive, loyal, humble, and innocent. They are extremely passionate about their loved ones, but they are also discriminating, which sometimes results in tumultuous relationships.

Ruling Planet: Mercury

Virgo is ruled by the planet Mercury. Mercury is known for its wit, intelligence, and chatty nature. Mercury is known as the messenger of Gods and thus handles a lot of information with precision and care. Virgo too handles information with care and ease. It is extremely skilled about information and can handle it meticulously by discarding the useless and accepting the useful. Virgo is extremely observant and analytical, thanks to the power of Mercury. It is also sensible and trustworthy. It is a great ally, thanks to its acute sense of knowledge.

Ruling House: 6th House of Routine

Virgo is the sixth sign of the zodiac, and it rules the sixth sign of the birth chart as well. The sixth house of the birth chart is the House of Routine. This house is concerned with your day-to-day life, your daily habits, your work, wellness, and personal growth. Virgo loves routine and structure. It is known for making intricate patterns. It is focused and bold.

Element: Earth

Virgo is ruled by the element of Earth. Earth stands for reliability, which makes Virgo such a dependable sign. Virgo is practical and observant. It understands its surrounding world properly and knows immediately if there is something different or wrong. It will notice even the tiniest detail that is out of place. Earth is concerned about the ground reality and is always aware of what happens around it. Similarly, Virgo lives in the present. Virgo loves routine and the cyclic aspect of nature, which represented by the element of Earth.

Color: Brown & Green

Mother Earth is represented by green and brown, so it is no wonder that her daughter, Virgo, is represented by the same shades. Virgo loves these natural shades. Brown, like the very soil on which everything stands, represents stability and focus. Virgo is closely associated with the harvest, so the golden-brown shade of ripe wheat also represents it perfectly.

Along with brown, Virgo adores green. Green is the color of growth and development. This represents Virgo's desire for personal growth and improvement. We are almost always surrounded by green, which represents Virgo's connection with its surroundings and atmosphere.

Quality: Mutable

Virgo is the last zodiac sign of the summer season. In this period, the hot and sweaty days are almost over, and Virgo uses its Mutable energy to bring the season to a close. Virgo loves planning and structure. These two things help Virgo to prepare everyone for change and new beginnings. Virgo is the harbinger of cool weather and new harvest.

Libra

Libra is one of the fairest, gracious, and balanced signs of the zodiac. It is also extremely popular and social, which makes it really popular among its peers.

Libra is ruled by Venus and is thus concerned with love and partnership. It is a considerate sign that cares for the needs of other people. It has an innate sense of what is wrong and what is right, which makes it fair and honest. Libra is concerned with the idea of justice and truth. It is the sign of balance, and thus it pays close attention to both the heart and the head. They understand that without logic, emotions are useless, and without emotions, logic is too practical. They love the desire and mutual feelings that are present in relationships, which makes them great lovers. Libras are beautiful both on the inside as well as outside. Ultimately, Libra stands for elegance, harmony, balance, and equality.

Positive Traits

Libra is well known for its graceful and charming demeanor. It possesses a great sense of judgment, which allows it to know what is wrong and what is right. It is fair and just, which makes it highly popular among people.

Negative Traits

Libra likes to look at both the side of every situation and object; this often makes them indecisive and slow. Sometimes their desire to look at all the facets of a situation can confuse them.

Advice

Libras love people. They always want to please them, but often they forget about their own needs while doing so. It is okay to be selfish sometimes.

Libra celebrities

Libras have been successful in many different fields. Some of the most famous Libras include Michelle Visage, Adore Delano, Kim Kardashian, Gwen Stefani, Hugh Jackman, Kate Winslet, Bruno Mars, Zach Galifianakis, Matt Damon, Zac Efron, etc.

Tarot Card: Justice

No surprises here. Libra is represented by the Tarot card of Justice. The Tarot card of Justice represents morals, truth, and fairness. It also represents the rights of human beings. It is firm, yet fair and encourages people to understand their actions and the results of their actions as well. In short, it stands for the law of karma. Libra is known for its sense of balance, and thus the card of Justice represents it well. Both of them are harmonious, fair, and observant.

Symbol: The Scales

Libra is represented by the Scales, which makes it a unique sign. All other signs of the zodiac are represented by something alive, while Libra is the only one that is represented by an inanimate object. It is true that many times, the Scales are held by a person, yet, the true symbol of Libra remains the Scales. The Scales stand for the notion of balance and harmony. Libra is always trying to find the balance of things in a fairway. Pound, the unit of measurement, is abbreviated as 'lb.' This 'lb.' is actually the abbreviation of the word 'Libra.' Libra is Latin for balance or scale.

Ruling Planet: Venus

Libra is ruled by the planet of love, Venus. It rules over Libra with the power of charm and persuasion. Libra is well known for being popular and smart. It is also graceful, pretty, and charming, thanks to Venus. As it is clear from the list of Libra celebrities, Venus blesses all those who are born under Libra with immense talent and beauty.

Ruling House: 7th House of Relationships

Libra is the seventh sign of the zodiac system, and it is the ruler of the seventh house, as well. The seventh house of the birth chart is the House of Relationship. This house is related to personal relationships and one to one relationships. It is mostly focused on romantic endeavors. Libra is graceful, fair, and empathetic. All these qualities are appreciated by their partners. They are also honest and kind, which makes them considerate about the needs, desires, emotions, and feelings of their partners.

Element: Air

Libra is governed by the element of Air. It is the element of Air that makes Libra firm. It also encourages it to be moralistic and ethical. Air is related to intelligence and clarity. Libra is blessed with both of these, which allow it to be just and honest. These two things allow Libra to maintain the balance of things. Libra is also the sign of peace and serenity like the sweet, light breeze. The sweetness of the Air makes Libra a calm and tranquil person.

Color: Pink & Light Blue

Libra is a soft and beautiful sign, so it is no wonder that it is represented by light blue and light pink. These simple, pale, and elegant shades make Libra seem fresh and likable. They represent the cool and serene nature of Libra. Light blue stands for the balanced, fair, and just side of Libra's attitude, whereas pink reflects its loving and sweet nature. Both these colors thus represent the innate qualities of this sign.

Quality: Cardinal

Libra is a Cardinal sign that falls in the fall season. It is the beginning of the fall. All Cardinal signs start a new season. Libra, for instance, starts the season of cool air and atmosphere. Libra is the seventh out of the twelve signs of the zodiac. Its position reflects its identity and attitude. It always strives for harmony and balance, and thus even in the sequence, it sits right in the middle. Another factor that represents Libra's quest for balance is the Fall Equinox, which takes place when the Sun enters Libra. On Equinox, the duration of the night and day are equal.

Scorpio

Scorpio is supposed to be one of the most mysterious, passionate, and deep signs of the zodiac. Scorpio is directly related to the underworld, and thus they prefer dark places. They consider such places homely and comforting. But unlike Cancer, it does not want to stay there forever because it prefers change and transformation. It is driven by the passion of exposing the truth or whatever that is hidden in the dark. Scorpios are passionate, and they are obsessed with depth, passion, answers, and questions. They think of life as a riddle that can be solved with proper methods. They rarely care for things that are superficial, and on the surface, Scorpios are more obsessed with what lies underneath. They are steadfast and intense. They believe that reinventing themselves and rebuilding themselves is their lifelong mission. They want to create the most intuitive and innovative self.

Positive Traits

Scorpio is intense and passionate. They have a charming and magnetic personality. They are intuitive and understand the minds of others.

Negative Traits

Scorpios are extremely passionate, almost to a fault. Their passion often overtakes their sensibilities. In romantic relationships, they can become controlling and jealous.

Advice

Scorpios are intense, and sometimes they can become a bit brash. It is recommended to avoid being too abrasive as it will not only hurt others, but it will also create problems for themselves as well.

Scorpio celebrities

Many famous celebrities are born under Scorpio. They include Ryan Reynolds, Emma Stone, Katy Perry, Ryan Gosling, Matthew McConaughey, Scarlett Johansson, Julia Roberts, Hillary Clinton, etc.

Tarot Card: Death

Don't be scared; the card of Death does not literally mean death. Scorpio's connection with this card symbolizes its connection with transformation and the cyclic nature of things. This card uses death as a metaphor for endings and new beginnings. It represents the end of projects, relationships, ideas, phases, situations, etc. It also represents the impermanence of things. Remember, not all endings are negative. Scorpio acts upon the impermanence of things and uses it to grow continuously. It does not care about killing off relationships, ventures, things, activities, prospects, etc. if it does not find them useful. Scorpios believe in the Kondo Method, where you need to remove things to make space for new ones. The Death card represents this. Some things need to die in order to allow new things to be born.

Symbol: The Scorpion

The Scorpio is represented by the Scorpion. Its glyph often shows a pointed arrow that represents the Scorpion's sting. Scorpions are often small, but they possess the vicious sting and a body as strong as armor. They are true warriors as they can attack as well as defend themselves with ease. Scorpions live in the dark and prefer solitude. Scorpios too adore dark and prefer solitude to other things. They can live and survive in uncomfortable situations with ease.

Scorpions would rather kill themselves than being killed, a trait that is reflected in Scorpios as well. Scorpions and Scorpios both love change and transformation.

Ruling Planet: Pluto

Scorpio is ruled by the planet Pluto. Pluto is powerful, strong, and persuasive. According to Roman myths, Pluto is supposed to be the Lord of the Underworld. This represents the planet's passion, depth, and intensity. It also represents its connection with the death. It is clear that Scorpio is closely associated with death and change. Pluto itself is related to death and rebirth. This cycle plays an integral part in Scorpios' overall life and attitude. Scorpios love to undergo metamorphosis.

Ruling House: 8th House of Intimacy

Scorpio is the eighth sign of the zodiac and rules the eighth house of the birth chart as well. The eighth house of the birth chart is the House of Intimacy. This house stands for things that we love and are passionate about. These things include everything personal, our values, our secrets, and physical intimacy as well. Scorpios do not care about superficiality; they like to understand what resides on the inside. They try to relate to others in profound and deep ways. They like to set their roots inside people and understand them properly.

Element: Water

Scorpio is a Water sign, i.e., it is governed by the element of Water. This element flows in a clear stream through Scorpio. Scorpios are emotional, intuitive, and passionate. They get these qualities from the element of Water. They also tend to prioritize emotions over brains, which again is derived from the element of Water. Underground water is often pure and clear thanks to the Earth's minerals. Similarly, Scorpios possess a golden heart and can undergo drastic transformation by searching deep inside.

Color: Black

Continuing the macabre and dark nature of Scorpio, the sign is ruled by the color black. Black is known for mysteries and darkness. It absorbs light. In many cultures, black is the color of death and funeral. This once represents Scorpio's potential of death and rebirth. It also reflects its potential for transformation.

Quality: Fixed

Scorpio is a fixed sign. It falls around the middle of the fall when the days become shorter and darker. These days are most suited for Scorpio. Fixed signs are self-aware and consistent. Scorpios know their powers and use them accordingly. When life slowly starts disappearing from the surface of Mother Earth, understand that it is the time of Scorpio. Scorpio, with its talents, dedication, and energy, pushes through these difficult days with ease. While it enjoys the darkness, it also reminds us of the imminent spring that will soon follow. It thus once again reflects its quality of transformation.

Sagittarius

Sagittarius is a sign obsessed with opportunity and growth. Many people born under this sign consider themselves to be eternal students, and they always seek knowledge through various sources, including traveling, books, people, life-lessons, ideas, etc. Sagittarius is obsessed with adventure and is always on a lookout for new ones. They have an extroverted or outgoing personality and a desire for the exotic and unknown. They are like a gigantic sponge that just wants to soak up everything that comes their way. The driving force behind Sagittarius is their constant desire to expand their hearts and mind by exploring and through adventure. They are well known for being fiery and independent, and no one can control them. The only thing that can limit them is their own mind and personality.

Positive Traits

Sagittarius is always ready for adventure. Due to this, if you are friends with a Sagittarius, you will never be bored. Sagittarius loves talking about various things, but their conversation often shifts to profound questions. They are outgoing and extremely friendly.

Negative Traits

Sagittarius, as said earlier, are extremely outgoing, and they love adventure. This often makes them a bit reckless- physically as well as vocally. Many people born under Sagittarius often hurt others without any intention of doing so. They are honest almost to a fault, and their blunt honesty and slightly carefree attitude can often lead to problems for others and themselves as well.

Advice

Sagittarius is hungry for adventure and is always eager to try new things. This often makes them excited and bold. Sagittarius should learn how to calm down and relax once in a while. This will allow them to enjoy the simplicity of life.

Sagittarius celebrities

Many well-known actors and singers are born under Sagittarius as these careers allow them to have constant adventures. Some examples include Britney Spears, Brad Pitt, Taylor Swift, Chrissy Tiegen, John Lennon, Miley Cyrus, Nicki Minaj, Samuel L. Jackson, Jay-Z, Walt Disney, Steven Spielberg, Ben Stiller, and Jake Gyllenhall.

Tarot Card: Temperance

The Temperance card represents Sagittarius perfectly. It represents understanding and wisdom. Tempering means finding the middle ground by combining all the best things from all the sides to create a strong force that can tackle anything. Sagittarius is capable of bringing philosophical strength into the physical world.

Symbol: The Archer

Sagittarius is represented with the Archer symbol. An arrow (sometimes bow with an arrow) is used to represent the Archer. The Archer represents Sagittarius's desire to explore new horizons and go on new adventures. Like the Archer can concentrate on a faraway target, Sagittarius too can focus and shoot a faraway goal with ease and precision. They are focused on learning new things, doing more activities, and seeing the world.

Ruling Planet: Jupiter

Sagittarius is a sign that has a larger than life personality, so it is no surprise that it is ruled by the largest planet in the solar system- Jupiter. Jupiter is believed to be the planet of expansion and luck. According to Roman mythology, Jupiter is supposed to be the king of gods and is thus supposed to be the best of all. According to astrology, Jupiter is supposed to be a 'benefit' planet. This means that Jupiter is the most opportunistic and the luckiest planet of all. Jupiter stands for positivity, which is reflected in Sagittarius's outgoing nature, its enlightened personality, and optimism. Sagittarius are so optimistic they often make people who come in their contact optimistic as well. As Jupiter is huge, it encourages Sagittarius to expand its horizons, mind, and heart.

Ruling House: 9th House of Expansion

Sagittarius is the ninth sign of the zodiac, and it rules the 9th house as well. The 9th house is the House of Expansion. This house represents openness, progressiveness, and our desire to expand our minds and personality. While there are many different ways to expand and enhance our personality and mind, some of the most common ones include education, life-lessons, adventures, and explorations. The 9th house encourages people to check out things and gain new experiences all the time. These things include philosophical conversations and debates, traveling, reading, explorations, etc. The ruler of the 9th house and the 9th house both are obsessed with growth, adventure, and desire for awareness. The 9th house and Sagittarius truly complement each other very well.

Element: Fire

Sagittarius is ruled by the element of fire. The element of Fire is essential as it represents ideas, thoughts, and the profound questions that arise in our minds. Sagittarius is often swayed by its element, and just like fire, it happily follows the course of life. It is always ready for adventure and often goes out of its way to seek and experience one. Fire represents the lifelong desire for exploration in Sagittarius. A Sagittarius loves trying new things and is always ready for the next adventure. The element of Fire is also responsible for their endless hope and optimism.

Color: Purple

Purple is a rich, exotic, and luscious color, which represents Sagittarius. Purple has been associated with abundance since ancient times. It makes Sagittarius try its luck and forces it to explore the world and expand its mind. Purple is traditionally associated with royalty, but it is also the color of enlightenment and spirituality. These two qualities make Sagittarius knowledgeable and smart. They also drive Sagittarius's interest in spirituality and philosophy.

Quality: Mutable

Sagittarius is the last sign of autumn. It is often thought to be the last sign of celebration as, after this, a long period of hibernation begins. Sagittarius loves change and variety. It uses its Mutable energy to shake some sense in the world and help it change. As said earlier, it is a Fire sign. All Fire signs keep us inspired by fueling our desire for fun throughout the cold days of winter. A combination of Mutability with Fire makes Sagittarius optimistic and positive.

Capricorn

Capricorn can be easily explained in three words, cool, steady, and calculating. Capricorn loves success and loves working hard for it, as well.

Capricorn is extremely goal-oriented and will do anything to achieve their goals. They use a combination of power determination, raw emotions, and their traditional methods to achieve their goals. While Capricorns can be conservative, they are also immensely caring, which makes them a great leader. Capricorns are dedicated, and they love their work.

Positive Traits

Capricorn can do anything for people they love. They not only care for them but can also defend them from attacks. They love to take care of others materially.

Negative Traits

Capricorns are extremely goal-oriented and hardworking. While these two things are great for their personal growth, they may make them neglect their friends and family as well. Many Capricorns are known to be quite rigid and do not like to display their feelings.

Advice

Capricorns need to be more appreciative and flexible. They should understand that while goals are important, friends, family, and personal relationships matter too.

Capricorn celebrities

Some famous Capricorn personalities are Bradley Cooper, Betty White, David Bowie, Liam Hemsworth, John Legend, Denzel Washington, Orlando Bloom, Martin Luther King Jr and Elvis Presley

Tarot Card: The Devil

Don't worry; The Devil is not a negative card. The Devil stands for the desire for success and the cycle of never-ending tasks. The Devil is represented in many ways in Tarot decks; the most common version includes picture Pan, the God of the Forests, reigning over hell. Capricorn always wants to succeed and reach the top of the ladder by any means. This positive trait can often turn negative for them. They may get trapped in a hell of their own making. The Devil represents this personal hell.

Symbol: The Mountain Goat

The Mountain Goat is the symbol of Capricorn. Mountain goats are incredible animals who can climb impossibly steep heights and cliffs with ease. They are enthusiastic, determined, and passionate. Like the Mountain goat, Capricorn is extremely determined as well. Once they set up their goal, they will continue to strive hard until they reach the top.

Ruling Planet: Saturn

Saturn is the ruler of Capricorn. In Roman mythology, Saturn is supposed to be the god of time and space. In astrology, Saturn stands for lessons, limits, and time. Saturn, when in full-effect, brings out the traditional side of Capricorn. It makes it practical, bold, and calculative. Saturn is often considered to be the planet of karma. This means that if you put in proper efforts, you will definitely win and succeed.

Ruling House: 10th House of Career

Capricorn is the 10th sign of the zodiac, and it rules over the 10th house as well. This house is supposed to be the house of career. It represents ambitions, career goals, public status, and relationship with the authority. Capricorn is obsessed with success for which it can do anything. This desire is represented well in this house.

Element: Earth

The element of Earth rules Capricorn. It makes it disciplined, committed, and hard-working. It also makes it reliable. Capricorn is a responsible sign, thanks to the element of Earth. The element of Earth allows Capricorn to take extra efforts and form proper plans and strategies to succeed in life.

Color: Grey & Brown

Brown and grey are the colors of Capricorn. These colors are strong neutral. They represent Capricorn's reliability, solidity, and traditional nature. Grey is the combination of two extremes i.e., black and white. This makes Capricorn neutral, conservative, and traditional. Brown is the color of Earth, and it stands for stability and determination.

Quality: Cardinal

Capricorn is a Cardinal sign. The beginning of Capricorn often marks the beginning of the winter season as well. It represents new beginnings. It is also the sign of 'New Year.' The Cardinal energy of Capricorn makes it energetic and full of hope and determination.

Aquarius

Aquarius is surely the strangest, quirkiest, and often the weirdest sign of the zodiac. They love to march to the beat of their own drum and hate being directed. It is an Air sign that is well known for being intellectual, unique, and social. They love mankind and society and want to do something for them. Aquarius prefers ideas to emotions. They possess stimulating and 'fun' personality, which makes them really popular with people. They are progressive and always strive for the greater good. They are also rebellious and a harbinger of change if they do not like something. Aquarius considers the head more important than the heart. They are visionary, brilliant, and inspiring.

Positive Traits

Aquarius is full of ideas and plans. They love fun and talking with others. They are also extremely helpful and can go out of their way to help someone.

Negative Traits

While Aquarius is friendly, they are also detached and aloof. This is why while Aquarius may have a lot of friends, they rarely develop close friendships. They are rarely intimate, which family and friends often find intimidating.

Advice

Aquarius is obsessed with acquiring knowledge. It becomes almost like an eternal quest for them, which can drive them crazy. Aquarius should relax once in a while and calm down a bit.

Aquarius celebrities

Some famous Aquarians are Justin Timberlake, Ellen DeGeneres, Oprah Winfrey, Jennifer Aniston, Alicia Keys, Abraham Lincoln, and Harry Styles

Tarot Card: The Star

The Star stands of optimism and hope. It is the harbinger of healing, inspiration, and idealistic energy. It allows Aquarius to plan everything perfectly to create their own perfect world.

Aquarius love to help people achieve their goals. They are also focused on the future. Both these things are supported by The Star.

Symbol: The Water-Bearer

While Aquarius is an Air sign, it is represented by a Water bearer. In this sign, a water bearer replenishes the water in the universe by pouring it out continuously from a jug. The symbol represents nourishment and cleansing. It stands for destroying all the falsifications and close-mindedness and replacing them with goodwill and the idea of community. As said earlier, the Aquarius is obsessed with knowledge and pours out the acquired knowledge in the world, just like its symbol pours water from his jug.

Ruling Planet: Uranus

Uranus is the ruler of Aquarius, and as the sign, it is rebellious as well. Uranus is considered to be the planet of surprise and change. It makes people react. It is a unique planet, just like the sign, because unlike other planets, it spins on a horizontal axis while all other spins on a vertical axis. Uranus provides Aquarius with a sense of creation, progression, and invention. It also makes it wise and powerful.

Ruling House: 11th House of Groups & Visions

Aquarius is the ruler of the 11th house. This house is the House of Groups and Visions. This house represents your relationship with humanity, society, people, and the things that inspire you. It also represents your ideals and visions that you want to achieve. Aquarius is well known for being open-minded and progressive; the 11th house inspires it to be so.

Element: Air

As said earlier, the symbol for Aquarius is the Water bearer. However, it is not ruled by the element of Water, rather it is ruled by the element of Air. The element of Air stands for ideas and intellect; this makes Aquarius extremely smart, brilliant, and innovative. People born under Aquarius can think quickly, create theories, make plans, and innovate almost at the speed of light. Their mind is rarely at rest, and it never sleeps. Once Aquarius starts thinking of something, they won't stop until they form a concrete plan.

Color: Blue

The Aquarius is closely connected to the color blue. Its symbol is the Water bearer, which is often painted in blue as well. Blue is the color of the sea and the sky, both of which stand of vastness. Like the sea, blue is also smooth and deep. Blue stands of the Aquarius's continuous flow of ideas and conversation. Blue can also help Aquarius to calm down a bit. Aquarius can be quite restless, but the color blue will mellow them down significantly. It should not come as a surprise that the ruling planet of Aquarius, Uranus, is also blue.

Quality: Fixed

Aquarius is the second sign of the winter season. It is a fixed sign that helps you to tackle the longest and coldest day of the year. Fixed signs are well known for their consistency and strength. These two factors allow Aquarius to be determined and focused. It also provides them with the courage to march on, even while facing immense opposition.

Pisces

Pisces are sensitive, dreamy, and have an affinity towards spiritualism. They are famous for being exceptionally emotional and are full of empathy and compassion. Due to this, they often put others' needs before theirs. Pisces are creative with deep souls. They love to live in a world of fantasy where they can let their imaginations fly. They know how to balance the practicality of the real world with a passion for understanding and love.

Positive Traits

Pisces are exceptionally sensitive and compassionate. They are great at empathizing with people and love people.

Negative Traits

Pisces can be dreamy, which often creates problems where they forget the difference between reality and fantasy. They are also prone to escapism, which may lead to negative habits, including alcohol dependency, drugs, etc.

Advice

Everyone loves to dream, but you should let your imagination take over your reality. Always your feet grounded in the real world and be practical as well.

Celebrities

Adam Levine, Rihanna, Jessica Biel, Drew Barrymore, Bruce Willis, Jon Hamm, Kurt Russell, Queen Latifah, Albert Einstein, Kurt Cobain are some well know Piscean celebs.

Tarot Card: The Moon

The Moon is an idealistic and mystical card. It is the ruling card of Pisces because Pisces are well known for their intuitive powers. The Moon card believes that one should go with the flow of nature and should not go against it. Pisces follows this philosophy to the T.

Symbol: The Fish

Pisces is instantly recognizable thanks to its symbol consisting of two fish. These fish are linked together forever. Two fish are used to represent Pisces instead of one because they represent Pisces' ability to exist in the conscious and the subconscious world simultaneously.

Pisces is the last sign of the zodiac. The two fish swimming in opposite directions also stands for the cyclic nature of things.

Ruling Planet: Neptune

Neptune is well known for being dreamy and fantastical; these feelings represent Pisces perfectly. According to Roman mythology, Neptune is supposed to be the God of the Sea, and like the sea, Neptune's influence on Pisces is deep and vast. Like the innumerable waves of the sea, Pisces flows through a sea of spirituality and imagination.

Ruling House: 12th House of Subconscious

The 12th house is supposed to be the House of Subconscious. Pisces rules this house. This house represents a person's emotions, spirituality, heart, and feelings. Pisces are supposed to be an intuitive sign; this is reflected in its house as well. This house represents contemplation and understanding, as well. It is the house of rejuvenation, reflection, and new beginnings.

Element: Water

It is obvious from the symbol of Pisces that its element must be water. The element of Water is present in every little detail of the sign. It is what makes it intuitive and empathetic. The element of Water is closely related to emotions, feelings, sensitivity, and spiritual connection. Pisces's heart is as deep and open as the ocean, which makes them loving and caring.

Color: Light Green

Light green can really work wonders with Pisces. It can improve the mystical nature of Pisces.

Green is the color of life. Thus, it represents Pisces's zeal to renewal. It inspires it to heal, rejuvenate, and help others. The softer the green, the better the results.

Quality: Mutable

Pisces is, in a way, the harbinger of spring. The cold, dark, and despicable winter start melting away slowly as soon as the season of Pisces begins. Pisces is a Mutable sign that desires change. All Mutable signs look out for changes and new things. Pisces also represents the end of the zodiac. This ending and Pisces's Mutable energy allows you to understand your position at the end of the year and helps you contemplate your next steps.

Chapter Five: Moon Signs and Ascendants

Moon Signs

As it is apparent, there are twelve signs of the zodiac. The position of the planets in all these signs and different houses is varied and unique for each person. The planets move continuously in the space.

The position of the Moon at the time of a person's birth determines his or her Moon sign. The Sun Sign is well known as most of the 'magazine' based astrology columns use it, but to understand a person's complete makeup, you need to know a lot more than their sun sign. Moon sign is one such thing.

Sun sign v/s Moon sign

The Sun is the most powerful object in the solar system, and thus it has the most profound and strong influence on a person. But this influence is mostly concerned with our external and physical personality. It does not say anything about our inner self and emotional makeup. The sun stays in each sign for around 30 days, so understanding a person thoroughly using just the sun sign is impossible and unreliable. It can often lead to inaccurate results and involves a lot of guesswork, as well. The Moon takes a considerably shorter time (i.e., 2.5 days only) to switch signs. This shorter duration allows us to understand the psychological, physical, and supernatural influences on our emotional makeup with added scrutiny. The Sun controls your external personality and how you depict it to the world, but the Moon represents your mind and inner self and thus represents what you truly are.

Many times, you may feel that people do not understand you. You perceive yourself in a different way as compared to other people. In simple words, your outer appearance often deceives people. This is why there are so many discrepancies between your Sun sign and your Moon sign.

The relevance of the Moon

The Moon sign is considered extremely important in many branches of astrology. This is due to the fact the Moon sign reflects your mind, your personality, and your emotional makeup. It also reflects your future. To calculate a Moon sign, you need to know the exact date, time, and birthplace of a person. This makes it more precise and detail-oriented than the Sun sign. The Moon represents our mind, feelings, and emotions. It represents how we act in situations. This makes the moon sign crucial. The Moon also controls our mood, and the waxing and waning of the Moon are often associated with mood swings.

The Moon is the closest planet to Earth, and it has a short revolution period of 28 days. The Moon is associated with femininity, motherhood, and the menstruation cycle, as well. The Moon, and in turn, the moon sign reflects our temperament, our instincts, our emotional makeup, our behavior, our interests, dislikes, and innate things. It is also related to our mental health and peace. Daily predictions and horoscope should ideally be based on the position of the Moon as it changes significantly every day.

The Sun sign reflects your outer personality. So, for instance, if you are a Cancer, you will appear to be homely, domestic, and lovable. But your moon sign will determine your true nature. So, if a person's sun sign is Cancer and their moon sign is Aquarius, then they will appear shy and lovable, but they will be truly iconoclastic, smart, and unique.

It is necessary to contact an astrologer or use online software to find your moon sign. Software and websites are reliable and are often available for free. It is recommended to find your moon sign before reading on further quickly.

Let us now have a look at how moon signs act differently than the sun sign.

Aries

Having the Moon in Aries is a curse and boon both. It can help them achieve great things but may leave them feeling emotionally drained and unsupported. Many times such people love sports and other such competitions because they often have defined winners and losers. This certainty provides them certain emotional outcomes as well. Many well-known lawyers have Aries as their moon sign.

Taurus

Taurus moons are pragmatic and emotional. They like to be practical while dealing with problems due to which they often move on or stop caring about things. Taurus develops a strong skin, and this armor-like skin makes it difficult for them to fall in love and for others to fall in love with them as well.

Gemini

Geminis are known for being absent, and this trait becomes even stronger when the Moon is in Gemini. They are talkative and often make tall claims that they cannot live up to. Their loquacious nature is often annoying for others. Even though they are chatty, they rarely reveal their true thoughts and emotions and keep them hidden. Many times they are out of touch with their feelings and emotions.

Cancer

People under the Cancer moon often have a difficult love life. They are indulgent about the past and love to wander around their old memories. They love nostalgia. They hate being insecure. When they are secure, they are some of the best people to be around, but if they ever feel insecure, they will act vicious and snarky.

Leo

Leos under the moon love to maintain decorum, but they struggle a lot. They may undergo a lot of emotional struggle constantly. They often guide others and assume the role of a leader. They have a lot of willpower and dedication. Their love for royalty and pride is quite apparent.

Virgo

Virgo moons are known for their quick wit, intellect, and a penchant for details. They do not feel obligated to things and traditions. They like to collect information from a lot of sources while doing projects. They often indulge in scholarly pursuits and love creating art as well. They are imaginative and creative. They can be a bit picky, which may turn off others quite often.

Libra

People often call moon Libras an airhead. Many Libras find it difficult to explain what they understand. Moon Libras are diplomatic, which is why they often second-guess things. This tendency is often seen as confusion and indecisiveness. Their emotional life is rich, and they love collecting information. Many times they are able to collect information that no one can see.

Scorpio

Having the Moon in Scorpio is great, as such people can understand the place and position of their emotions. By understanding their position, they can try to move and manipulate them. It is true that controlling emotions is difficult, but they can still fake it. Many Scorpio moons are experts at hiding their true feelings and appearing in public with a poker face. They can appear impassioned and disinterested, as well. They are certain about things, but their certainty can sometimes create a lot of problems, as well.

Sagittarius

Sagittarius is known for being adventurous and courageous. They love to take challenges and gambles with life. They may have a blunt personality, but they are not impenetrable. They love the world, and they want to have it all. Their personality is strange; they either want everything or they want nothing at all. Finding a soulmate is not difficult for them; sometimes, they may find their soulmates more than once.

Capricorn

Having the Moon in Capricorn can help people understand their place in the world and its workings, as well. They will never feel bored, as they will always know that they are a significant part of a large system. But Capricorns can often be status quo-ist. They do not like change. They are rarely flexible and do not like to turn things around. Navigating the modern world may be difficult for them as our world is changing constantly and rapidly.

Aquarius

Having Aquarius as your Moon sign is brilliant as it increases and enhances the person's mental activity. But on the downside, it takes away their personal touch. They become more practical and basic. They view themselves as a corporation and talk to others as if they are customers (and sometimes their competitors as well). They can work wonders in teams, but only as long as their interests are being met. They love being appreciated; however, thanks to their practical and dry nature, they may not have anyone to appreciate them. Their professional success may come at the cost of their personal failure.

Pisces

Having the Moon in your Pisces makes people sacrificial and lovable. They will always put others and their needs in front of them and their needs. For instance, in a professional setting, they will try to adjust their schedule according to the schedules of others. Such people are often escapists and love to dream. They are well known for being daydreamers.

Rising Signs and Ascendants

Along with your Moon sign and your Sun sign, your Ascendant sign matters a lot. Your Ascendant is also known as your rising sign. These are the signs that rise from the eastern horizon when you were born. It is often abbreviated as ASC or AS in birth-charts. You can calculate the exact degree of your ascendant if you know the exact time of your birth.

The position of the Ascendant is crucial. It becomes even more important when the Sun is weak in the birth chart (for instance, in the case of night birth).

Ascendants are completely dependent on the specific place and time of the birth of the individual. It thus represents the atmosphere and the conditioning that the child may get. Many people consider it even more important than the Sun and Moon signs.

The Ascendant is often compared with our 'outside' personality. It represents the first impression that we make while meeting new people. This is why many people find it strange when new people describe them. The ascendant can also influence your physical characteristics and traits. It gets reflected in your style, your image, your mannerisms, and the way you act as well. According to some modern astrologers, the effect of the ascendant grows weak with age.

Your rising sign is your first impression, while your Sun sign is your true representation. The rising sign is like the autopilot mode. The rising sign and the ascendant both combine together to form a complex outer shell under which the Moon sign resides comfortably. Let us now have a look at different ascendant signs and what they say about your personality.

Ascendants and Personality

By now you must have understood the traits and quirks of your Moon sign and Sun sign. Everyone loves checking their horoscope of the week in magazines, newspapers, etc. But many times, these horoscopes turn into 'horror scopes.' Similarly, many times, people display traits that are polar opposites of their sun-sign. For instance, a Cancer person who enjoys being the center of attention all the time is a bizarre situation. Why does this happen? Your sun-sign no doubt defines your character, but it is incomplete on its own. To understand the whole personality, you need to understand your moon sign and your ascendant thoroughly. In this section, let us have a look at all the ascendant signs one by one.

Calculating your Ascendant

Like Moon sign, you cannot calculate your perfect ascendant if you do not know your exact birthplace and time. To calculate your ascendant, use a free online service, as they are often easy to use and trustworthy. You can also contact an astrologer for this.

Meanings of Ascendants

Cancer

People often think that these people are shy when they meet them for the first time, but later they often say the opposite. Cancer ascendants are confusing and often befuddle people. Many people often believe Cancer ascendants to be quiet, reserved, and introverted. This is true, but as soon as people get to know them better, their sun sign comes through. Having a Cancer ascendant can be bad for their social life as people often confuse their reserved nature as being disengaged, standoffish, and egoistic. They should keep this in mind while meeting new people.

Leo

Leos are bold and confident. They love to be the center of attention. They love crowds and are often extroverted. They possess a crowd-pleasing attitude and the gift of gab. They are self-assured and possess a lot of self-esteem. They can handle a lot of stress without any problem and hesitancy.

Virgo

They are often socially anxious, and they despise new situations. They avoid large crowds, as they can be nerve-wracking. They are sensitive to criticism, and even off-handed comments and backhanded compliments can break them. They have great observational skills, and they can scrutinize a situation and people effortlessly. They are emotional, which may prove to be a huge problem while making new friends.

Libra

They are extremely charming and smart. They can flirt with anyone and are well known for their comforting presence and delightful aura. They love being a host or hostess and love parties, as well. They display ease and effortlessness, and people love them. They have a magnetic personality, and people always want to be friends with them.

Scorpio

Scorpios are mysterious, and an aura of mystery follows them all the time. They are well aware of this and love it. They are often flirtatious and bold. They are secretive and can be broody as well. They are intense and emotional, which many new people find off-putting and strange. Scorpios may seem to be too intense and 'dark.' These people should avoid showing too much of their true self while meeting new people or they may even scare them away.

Sagittarius

People with Sagittarius as raising signs are honest and open. People love them for having a positive aura. They are dependable and trustworthy. They don't keep their feelings hidden and express their opinions freely. These personal opinions can be about anything, including simple things such as music and literature, to more controversial things, including politics. They love a healthy debate but rarely get serious about it. Everything is in good fun for them.

Capricorn

Capricorns love groups and crowds. They adore speaking in public. They like meeting new people. People with Capricorn ascendants often have everything under control, and it is apparent to everyone around them. They appear confident and bold, which is why they often do well in interviews. They are not frivolous about emotions and finances. They can be a bit rigid sometimes and need to learn to let loose once in a while.

Aquarius

Aquarius ascendants can be confusing. People do not understand them in the first meetings (and sometimes they don't understand them after the 100th meeting as well.) They are a unique and one of a kind person. They are openly idealistic, and cynical-minded people may not appreciate them. But don't worry; their charm and friendly attitude will win everyone over. They are extremely curious and creative, which makes them popular with everyone. They do not find it difficult to make genuine connections with people.

Pisces

Pisces is slightly elusive but highly easygoing individuals. They are often major romantics. Sometimes they can seem to be too imaginative. They are compassionate and empathetic. They can understand peoples' feelings better than all other zodiacs. These qualities often make first interactions intense.

Aries

They are a party animal and love socializing a lot. They are probably into networking and partying. They love to make new connections and contacts all the time. They are a natural-born leader and have an impeccable sense of social skills. They are fearless and bold. Nothing can dampen their spirit. Just be sure that they do not attack others and dominate them with their overenthusiastic attitude.

Taurus

Taurus ascendants are calm, cool, and collected all the time. They have lots of grace and style but prefer to stay at home in their warm and cozy bed. They are friendly and high-spirited people.

Gemini

Gemini ascendants are curious and earnest. They love investigating new things. This trait makes them really popular with other people. They are blessed with the gift of gab, and thanks to their chatty and loquacious nature, they can make friends with anyone almost instantly. They are the perfect traveling companions. They love getting into crazy adventures with strangers and love the excitement derived from such encounters.

Chapter Six: The Four Elements

According to traditional science, there exist four natural elements that govern our body and soul. These elements also govern astrology and our life. These elements are Air, Fire, Water, and Earth. These elements have enjoyed an important position since ancient times. They were used and studied by alchemists and scientists who wanted to understand Nature. These four elements are considered to be the pillars on which our world resides. These elements also play a significant role in the system of the zodiac. In the next section, let us have a look at them one by one.

Zodiac and the Elements

All the signs of the zodiac belong to one of the four elements and display their characteristics. Knowing the elements of the zodiac signs can help us understand them in a better way. You can use them to understand the personality and attitude of individuals. It can also prove beneficial in understanding the compatibility of individuals and signs. For instance, Earth signs often do well with Water signs, and Fire and Air signs go together. This connection is based on logic as well because Water gives Earth life and fertility while Air keeps Fire burning bright.

Let us now have a look at all the four elements and their signs one by one.

The Air Element

The element of Air is important as it connects all the other elements and binds them together. It is often considered to be irrelevant to many people because it is invisible. But such people are mistaken, as they do not understand its importance. Air is far away from Earth, and it deals with mental planes and things that do not satisfy our earthly and physical needs. This element is found in almost everyone and everything. For instance, the Sun burns bright thanks to Hydrogen, which is a form of air. Without Fire, life would not have existed, and ultimately; Air is the reason behind life. This proves that for the survival of life, all the four elements are required.

The element of Air gives us a place to breathe and open our Soul. It makes us independent and gives us our personal freedom. All Air signs love to be independent, and they do not like to be controlled or ordered around.

Air Signs

The element of Air rules three signs viz. Gemini, Libra, and Aquarius.

People who are born under a strong element of Air often find it difficult to fit into their surroundings. This may include their family, their social circle, their workplace, or even their nation. Such people should stop pleasing others and instead focus on being happy and liberated.

How Do We Balance Air?

The most significant challenge an Air individual can face is finding grounding. Air signs often find it difficult to attach themselves. They prefer to stay in the 'higher spheres' and delve in the fantastical lands. For them, everything seems possible. They often get brilliant but impractical ideas. It is often difficult to implement their ideas into reality and use their knowledge and intelligence in the practical (or physical) world.

Air signs love to talk and gossip. They often are more verbal than physical. If they really want to succeed, Air signs should focus on practical aspects of life and start doing concrete things. The element of Air can be balanced by introducing the element of Earth in their life.

Earth can provide the much-needed grounding for Air signs. It also represents daily routine, which can help Air signs to stay active, healthy, and fit. It will also constantly remind them of their physical aspect, which they tend to forget sometimes. Thus, the element of Earth can help Air signs to understand their primal needs.

The Fire Element

The element of Fire is the only element out of the four that shines. No other element shine. Yes, the element of Water sparkles, but it can only sparkle by reflecting the light created by fire. Fire represents energy. Water too possesses a lot of energy, but its energy is weaker as compared to the element of Fire.

Fire Signs

The element of Fire rules three signs of the zodiac, which are Aries, Leo, and Sagittarius. These signs reflect the power of Fire and the strength of the Sun. People who are born under these sun signs should try to understand their emotional side along with their physical aspect. These signs often require training to be more compassionate about the needs of others. They are 'givers' and often give things to people who don't want them. This is especially true in romantic relationships where their constant presence can feel smothering and suffocating. All people born in this element use the spark for their own needs. They only use it for others when they are asked for some advice or help. Sagittarius is the most giving sign out of all the Fire signs.

How Do We Balance Fire?

Fire is a strong element that exerts masculine energy. But masculinity is incomplete without femininity. It often ignores the underlying feminine energy present in its core. A life without love is useless and not worth living. Fire signs need to learn how to appreciate love and emotions. They need to understand the worth of emotional bonds and should be encouraged to tap into their feelings. The element of Fire can be balanced with the feminine element of Water.

Fire signs, as the name suggests, can be fiery and brash. They need to understand the importance of controlling their feelings. They need to understand how to be calm and quiet. A peaceful and calm mind can help them use their energy in positive ways.

Fire signs always try to move forward by leaving others behind. People who have a lot of Fire in their birth chart often forget that sometimes defense is the best offense. Therapy and happiness can really work wonders with such charts. They can learn how to use their energy and excitement and store it for later use as well.

The Water Element

The element of Water is slow but steady, and it continuously moves around. It is mysterious and is present in all of us in various forms. Blood, tears, sweat, etc. everything is a form of water that resides in the dark but cozy places. This is the element of imagination, conception, illusions, mystery, fairy tales, secrets, Soul, and death. It is the element of the beginning and the element of the end, as well.

This element literally deals with matters of life and death. It is also the element of emotions and feelings. Our emotions are constant, which means they never die; they just pass one from person to person. All the emotions that we feel in our lives have been passed on to us by our ancestors. Water signs also represent motherhood and maternity.

Water Signs

The Water element rules three signs, which are Cancer, Scorpio, and Pisces. This element is slightly complicated because the ruler of Cancer is present in Scorpio. All three water signs are immensely emotional and are driven by their feelings. But embracing their true feelings is often difficult for these signs. These signs need to learn how to accept their negative aspects and sadness like they accept positivity and love.

Water signs are often considered to be too emotional. They often deal with a bombardment of suffering without even realizing that the suffering simply does not exist. They are sensitive, caring, and critical. These three qualities make them great therapists and advisors. They are also compassionate, which makes them patient listeners. They can help people solve deep and dark emotional problems. Their love is endless, and they often preach it to other people.

How Do We Balance Water?

People who are born under the element of Water need to understand and use their emotions properly. This element has a lot of potential, perhaps the most potential than any other element, but it is also lazy and often avoids expressing itself. Known for their creativity and talent, Water signs can change the world if they can get out of their beds. Water is an amalgamation of all the knowledge and talent of the world, and it gives it out freely.

Water stands for an endless pool of potential and possibility, but being a pool, it becomes almost impossible for signs to find a direction. The only way to solve this problem is by countering it with the element of Fire. Fire can help these people and can become their guiding light. It will give them ample energy, direction, and passion. It will show them where and how their talents can be useful. Fire combined with Water can help them create things effortlessly. Water will carry them from shore to shore and bank to bank, but if they ever want to reach a harbor, they need to include Fire in their life. Else, they will continue to spin in circles endlessly and will never find direction or a way out.

The Earth Element

The element of Earth is a powerful element as it forms the base of all the other elements. It stands for our existence and the realization of our dreams and missions. The Earth is considered to be a complex element as it is unmovable, stiff, and stable. If a person has a lot of planets in the Earth element and very few in the Air element, then their birth chart often becomes too stiff.

The element of Earth, as the name suggests, is the element of our planet. It is necessary for every birth chart as, without this element, people may find it difficult to find their grounding. Such people are also 'rootless' which means they do not get attached to a place, including their hometowns as well.

Earth Signs

The element of Earth rules three signs, which include Capricorn, Virgo, and Taurus. All these signs are practical and materialistic. They prefer the comfort of life and will work hard for it. They are great at planning things and always plan for success. All the above signs can be specific, concrete, and practical. They often want others to share their practical point of view, which may or may not be appreciated.

The Earth represents our physical body, the food we eat, our finances, and our day-to-day routine. All Earth signs are set in their ways and rarely change. Many individuals do not even change their routine for years together. Many times they avoid changes because they are scared of beginning anew. Even while facing challenging situations, they prefer to stick to their habits even if they do not make them happy. They believe that if they leave, they may lose something significant. Many times their stubborn nature affects their creativity and intelligence in a negative manner.

How Do We Balance Earth?

Earth signs are stiff and fixed. If they want to change, then they must shake off things and make changes in their routines and lives. These changes can seem to be daunting and difficult at first, but with the time you will get used to them. Do not regret things when you change them. Being a status quo has never helped anyone. You need to stop questioning yourself and stop questioning your decisions, as well. Have a clear sense of purpose and be in touch with your feelings and emotions. These things may take special efforts, especially for Virgo (who is ruled by Venus), but with the time you will get used to it. Earth is directly countered by the element of Air. If you introduce the element of Air in your life, you will automatically cut down some of the negative traits associated with Earth. For instance, start socializing and going on coffee with others. Be as random as possible, and go for frequent walks. Try reading fantasy and similar genres. Watch movies and talk to people about them. Be ambitious, bold, and bright. Try to be chatty as well. Keep your body fit by incorporating stretching and yoga in your daily schedule. Many people born under the element of Earth love dancing.

Chapter Seven: Cardinal, Fixed, Mutable (Quadruplicities)

Quadruplicity stands for a group of four. In astrology, this often refers to the group of three qualities in which all the twelve signs have been divided equally. These three qualities are Cardinal, Fixed, and Mutable. As the name suggests, these three groups define the qualities of the sign. Let us have a brief look at all these groups one by one.

Cardinal

The word 'cardinal' is derived from the French word 'cardo.' It means a hinge on which things turn, e.g., a door hinge. The door is important, but without the hinge, it is useless. Cardinal signs are the signs when the seasons change. There are four cardinal signs that represent all the four seasons (and changes). All these signs are the harbinger of new beginnings and change. In astrology, the firs, the fourth, the seventh, and the tenth sign are considered to be cardinal. All these signs are the symbols of new beginnings.

Sometimes these four signs, i.e., Aries, Libra, Cancer, and Capricorn, are divided into two groups. These groups are the equinox signs consisting of Aries and Libra, and the solstice group consisting of Cancer and Capricorn. Equinox is the day on which both night and day enjoy the equal time. Cancer solstice is the longest day in the Northern hemisphere, and Capricorn solstice is the longest night. Aries and Libra are known to be the times of balance. They are also known as the times of abrupt and sudden change. Cancer and Capricorn represent the times of extremes.

Cardinal signs are also known as enterprising because they begin new things. They are often aggressive and forceful about things that they want to accomplish. They love change and new beginnings. They project into the world. They are creative and imaginative and thus like to create new things and situations. All the four signs under the cardinal group do this differently. For instance

Aries will begin and create new things in an energetic and urgent manner. They can also be quite impatient. They hate waiting and are motivated by their enthusiasm.

They want to achieve whatever they have planned instantly and cannot wait to start the process.

Cancer is far more patient. They are well known for being emotionally assertive. They project emotions and feelings in a far more sensitive and protective manner. They can also be manipulative and indulge in it frequently to get what they want.

Libra is the sign of balance. They do everything in a balanced and justified manner. They will always try to consider all the sides of a situation before coming to a judgment. Libra is ruled by the element of Air, and they often project themselves through their mouth, i.e., verbally unlike Aries, who prefer to get physical right away. Libras are masters of language and use it for their benefit.

Capricorns are down to earth and highly practical. They like success and do things accordingly. Their down to earth persona is appreciated by people, and they often receive a lot of help from others.

Fixed Signs

Fixed means secured or fastened. The signs that are considered to be fixed do not like changes. In astrology, the second, the fifth, the eighth, and the eleventh signs i.e., Taurus, Leo, Scorpio, and Aquarius, are considered to be fixed. They enjoy stability. They are also dependable and firm in their decisions and choices.

All the fixed signs want to maintain things or change them in such a way that they assume their original state. These signs work hard to stabilize things. While change and fixed may appear contradictory, in astrology, they can often stand for the same things. For instance, if you want to keep your body healthy and stable, you need to 'change' it frequently. These changes include feeding it, cleaning it, and taking proper care of it. If you do not feed your body regularly, it will not remain stable. Thus, appearances can be deceiving. A lot of times, changes hide under the surface of stability, and without these changes, stability will collapse on itself.

Let us now look at the four fixed signs one by one.

Taurus is the first fixed sign. Taurus is obsessed with making personal things stable, fixed, and permanent. These things include material wealth, physical health, etc. Taurus hate changing their wealth. They are obsessed with it. Many Taurus people feel threatened when their personal wealth gets affected.

Leo is far more obsessed with personal power. They like to be the center of attention and want everyone to think that they are creative and impressive. Leos often make different changes to stay in power.

Scorpio is fixed regarding their emotions and feelings. They feel secure and happy when they know what feelings the other people have. Scorpio only makes changes when it is trying to search for deep emotions and feelings. These two factors motivate them.

Aquarius, on the other hand, like to stick to their beliefs and ideas regarding a lot of things, including humanity. Aquarius like to keep their friends stable. Similarly, if they love revolutions and thrill, they will continue to seek thrill and be revolutionaries for the rest of their lives.

Mutable Signs

'Mutable' stands for 'subject to change.' All the signs in this group are adaptable, and they can change themselves according to the need and requirements of the time. This group includes the third i.e., Gemini, the sixth i.e., Virgo, the ninth i.e., Sagittarius, and the twelfth i.e., Pisces signs of the zodiac.

Mutable signs love changing things into something else. This includes transforming and moving on, as well. Fixed signs do not like change, but mutable signs appreciate it. Mutable signs are the last signs of each cycle, and they give rise to Cardinal sign of the next cycle. All mutable signs are considered to be double signs. Let us have a look at all of them one by one.

Gemini is ruled by the element of air, and therefore it is closely associated with words, communication, and mind. Geminis often adapt themselves to their surroundings effortlessly. Fixed signs often change the environment to fit their liking, while Gemini and similar signs change themselves. For instance, if a Scorpio cannot find its favorite food in a restaurant, it will change the restaurant or force the staff to make it, but if a Gemini cannot find its favorite food, it will change its tastes and find a new favorite food instead. Geminis and other mutable signs can adapt and change quickly whenever it is necessary. This does not mean that they are untrustworthy and that they change all the time like a chameleon. Mutable signs too can resist change (or try to change the environment instead of themselves). However, this happens only when there exists no other option.

Virgo is an analytical and critical sign. They often analyze situations and find the problems with it. They hate falsity.

Sagittarius is the ninth sign of the zodiac. It is ruled by the element of fire. They seek truth and destroy ignorance.

The last sign of the zodiac is Pisces. It tries to change and adapt its emotions. It prefers being one with things.

Conclusion

Once again, thank you for buying this book, and I hope you found it interesting and informative.

Astrology is one of the most exciting subjects in the world. It is delicate and is related to the human psyche and the stars above us. Understanding astrology and using it in our day-to-day lives can help you achieve your goals with ease.

This book contains all the essential information that is required to understand astrology and zodiac. It contains a detailed chapter on the planets in astrology and how they are important if you want to understand astrology properly. It also contains three chapters on Sun Signs, Moon Signs, and Ascendant signs. These signs are crucial to understanding a person's personality. This book also features a detailed chapter on the birth chart and how to read them. Many astrologers proclaim that knowing your moon sign, ascendant, and another couple of things is necessary if you want to understand your real personality. It also features detailed sections on the qualities of the signs and the elements that govern our houses.

Once again, thank you for buying this book, and I hope it will help you in your future life.

Reference

https://en.wikipedia.org/wiki/Planets_in_astro
logy

https://en.wikipedia.org/wiki/Astrological_sign

https://www.indastro.com/planet-sign/sun-
sign.html

https://www.tarot.com/astrology/zodiac

https://www.indastro.com/moon-sign/moon-
sign.html

https://www.keen.com/articles/astrology/astrol
ogy-moon-sign

https://www.alwaysastrology.com/rising-
signs.html

https://www.brit.co/wedding-beauty/boho-
wedding-dress

https://entertainment.howstuffworks.com/horo
scopes-astrology/horoscope1.htm

https://www.allure.com/story/12-astrology-
houses-meaning

https://www.astrology-zodiac-signs.com/astrology/elements/

https://trans4mind.com/personal_development/astrology/LearningAstrology/quadruplicities.htm

Made in United States
Troutdale, OR
12/20/2023

16240721R00086